A WORLD SOLD ON IMAGE

THE TRUTH ABOUT REAL BEAUTY

LISA D'ANNA

ISBN: 978-1-7372688-0-2

Library of Congress Control Number: 2021910412

Printed in the United States of America

Website: www.Lifestyleofbeauty.com

DEDICATION

To my husband, who I'm lucky enough to call my best friend, and who I swear is an angel. Thank You for loving me at my worst and celebrating with me at my best. This book would not have happened without you.

To my grandparents, You will never know the impact you made not only on my life but on my very soul. I hope you two are 'jitterbugging' away in eternity.

To my daughter, who taught me the true meaning of unconditional Love. May you never let that bright light of yours dim.

To my mother, thank you for giving me life and guiding me. I know that's you.

CONTENTS

INTRODUCTION

WHY I WROTE THIS BOOK

WHEN I SAY I LOVE THE COSMETIC AND FASHION WORLD, I mean, I LOOOOVVVE it!

We are forever in its debt for fabulous high heels, classic red lipstick, and those versatile concealers that cover everything from blemishes and redness to those dreaded dark under-eye circles.

I'm obsessed with all the lotions and all the potions. The cosmetic industry is a place where the real magic happens. It's astonishing how a dynamic red lipstick and a multilevel mascara can turn a shy, timid kitten into a fierce, growling lioness, ready to take on the wild—and all within minutes.

The cosmetic and fashion industries draw the most splendorous and diverse personalities in the world together because they offer a creative space that encourages self-expression. It's a place where anyone can unwind, experiment with cosmetics that enhance their best features, try on the latest fashion trends, and make themselves feel like a runway model. At least for a little while, one can create confident, feel-good energy all around. When people are surrounded by others who feel comfortable and attractive, they can't help but feel a sense of that confidence within themselves.

However, for many people, confidence can fizzle fast. It fades during the drive home, then disappears as soon as they jump back on to social media, where they are reminded that there are far better-looking people in the world. So, they retreat to their self-judging self-talk. *Who am I kidding? I'll never be enough.*

Why is this?

Much of our self-sabotage comes from focusing our attention on unrealistic images, which claim that this look "creates beauty" or that look "is slimming." It isn't surprising, as millions of dollars go into marketing and sales training to exploit the insecurities of target demographics. This industry has wholly hijacked what it means to be *beautiful* and taken the liberty to define it as sex appeal—an image that is constantly changing, which only serves to keep women feeling insecure and companies' pockets growing fat.

They say to be beautiful; we *MUST* look a certain way.

Welcome to the dark side of the cosmetic and fashion industries. DUN DUN DUN… They bombard us twenty-four seven with an abundance of advertising containing fashion models with bodies which only 0.0001% of the population can achieve (often with the help of a plastic surgeon). If these companies keep shoving unattainable goals in front of our beautiful faces, we'll have to spend more money to chase them. They know this. They bank on this.

Cosmetic and fashion businesses know humans are hardwired to seek sex appeal. Most advertising—even for products that have nothing to do with fashion or cosmetics—targets the primal parts of our brains because our primal brain is the first line of defense. It's the survival mechanism part of the brain. It immediately distinguishes whether something is desirable or threatening. The primal brain controls involuntary functions like heartbeat, fear, and sexual desires (or mating). Marketing stimulates this part of the brain with overtly sexual photos intent on creating enough arousal to compel an impulse buy before the rational part of our mind kicks in and questions our reasoning.

Primal marketing has us intentionally look through a distorted lens that will capture what *they* think makes a woman beautiful. It makes the buyer question the positive thoughts she may have about herself since she *clearly* doesn't fit the overly sexualized look of the images on her screen. She may find herself thinking, *Well, maybe I'm not beautiful after all.*

There is no reason a 14-year-old with perfect skin should want an extra, extra, extra coverage foundation or contemplate Botox! Ahh! Yes, this is happening, and it's constantly happening in every state and city worldwide. These girls are not trying to cover anything on their faces or trying to be sexy for themselves; they are trying to keep up with the virtual world's forever-changing definition of beauty.

Why is the definition of beauty constantly changing?

It's forever changing because it becomes common once EVERYONE looks like you, and change instantly creates the opportunity for companies to sell new products. If we follow their trends, we constantly need a fresh look to feel different and validated.

Genuine beauty is constant.

These companies have erased what it means to be beautiful because once a person discovers this truth, their focus on image quickly fades along with the amount of money they are willing to spend on products.

I'm here to tell you RIGHT HERE. RIGHT NOW: Companies and their employees are stressed daily trying to meet quotas. They need to sell a certain number of products to stay in business or to keep their jobs. I've been there and done that. I worked as a national brand representative for several cosmetic brands. Those brands need to be the ones to shape the definition of beauty. If *you* have the correct definition of beauty, you won't buy theirs. To feel good about ourselves and be the best versions of ourselves, we should strive to be attractive, but on our terms, in a healthy way, and with a HUGE reminder that attractiveness and sex appeal are NOT BEAUTY. I repeat how you look has nothing to do with the constant of beauty—who you are!

You are the beauty.

INIMITABLE BEAUTY. No one else can or will ever be able to duplicate it. Period. It drives me crazy that the word beauty gets used so carelessly. There are many attractive people in this world that I would never, ever define as beautiful.

Poet and philosopher Ralph Waldo Emerson once said, "The love of beauty is taste. The creation of beauty is art." I love this quote so much, but I would reword it a bit. As stated above, I don't think we can create beauty. It is the constant of beauty that creates the art. We can experiment with our image and become more attractive, but it is the *spirit* of beauty inside every one of us that allows us to create and serve a purpose. Our purpose is the most beautiful thing about us. It is the one thing unique about us, and it is not for sale.

Companies can't sell us ourselves, so we have to want to be someone else.

When I contemplated the idea of writing a book, I imagined it would revolve around the latest and greatest anti-aging products—because, well, I'm obsessed with trying out different products. It always makes me feel pretty, and I have a fun time testing it all. I think we all have experienced the joy of finding those products that really work— those magical concoctions make us want to jump up and down and yell 'hallelujah' from the roof tops. However, after getting a behind-the-scenes look at what takes place before a cosmetic product gets sold and what some advertising is doing to young minds today, I soon discovered that I would embark on a different mission. I could talk all day about the best plumping lipstick and ravishing eye cream. I could recommend amazing products from all over the world, but all of that is useless if you're a beautiful 14-year-old girl or a stunning 40-year-old woman with an addiction to comparison and feeling worthless. Even after applying a pound of foundation to your face, you will remain dissatisfied because you're striving to become something that is only an image of false perfection. Cosmetics should enhance who you are, not change who you are. The pursuit of beauty should lead to elevated feelings of confidence and happiness. If you feel anything less, you're on the wrong path. You've bought into advertising.

"Never write an advertisement which you wouldn't want your own family to read. You wouldn't tell lies to your own wife. Don't tell them to mine. Do as you would be done by. If you tell lies about a product, you will be found out."
— David Ogilvy
(Advertising tycoon, founder of Ogilvy & Mather, and known as the "Father of Advertising")

The cosmetic industry shouldn't refer to itself as the *beauty industry* because you will never find genuine beauty there. The *illusionist industry* might be a more suitable term. It is a magical media show, and if you cast yourself in it without a strong sense of character, you risk concealing the essence of beauty that only you can bring into the world.

We need no more women killing themselves or damaging their souls to achieve the look of a plastic doll or the newest trend to feel valued. There is a unique, beautiful badass inside each of us waiting to shine through, but we drown out our inner voice to catch up with an image the media has created for us. When you take time to discover and embrace what makes you unique, you become more beautiful.

You will become more and more authentic, and authenticity is genuinely the only beauty you own. And the bonus? Real beauty doesn't age.

Wouldn't it be great to have fun with cosmetics again? The media's definition of beauty is short-lived. Real beauty is ever-lasting. However, discovering real beauty takes work. It is an inside job, and we need to let that truth sink in more profound than a feel-good foundation that says, *"Oh yeah, I'm beautiful. Got it."* We need to have an accurate understanding of why image is an obsession, what beauty is, and how we can become even MORE beautiful—and yes, yes, that includes looking YOUR best on the outside. I dedicate to you a chapter of my top ten products and practices for skin, hair, and mind toward the end of the book; all culminated from my years of experience in the industry. Thank you for taking the time to read this book. I hope it changes your mind about how beautiful you truly are.

Shine on,
Lisa D'Anna

CHAPTER ONE

WHY WE CORRELATE BEAUTY WITH AN IMAGE

IT STARTS YOUNG.

My first experience with image happened when I was five years old. I was on the playground monkey bars when my crush came over to play. Pumped to the brim with excitement and rushing adrenaline, I built up all five years of confidence I had and said to him, "I think you're cute." He said, "I think you're ugly." Yep! He straight-up called me ugly. Woah!

I wasn't crushed, just a little confused. This moment was my first encounter with *ugly* from a peer. I kid you not; my first thought was, "He must need glasses." I felt terrible for him. He was too cute to continue life with such impaired vision. Then, I moved on to think about how great I would look in glasses. A five-year-old's mind is awesome.

The beauty of being a kid is that you have no concept of what *ugly* and *pretty* really mean, confidence is sky high, and life is fun. It's a world in which "boys have cooties," and you pull their hair if you like them. It makes no sense, but you roll with it because it makes you laugh, and your confidence is unbreakable. Besides, there was *NO WAY* I could be ugly because my family, the photographer on school picture day, and my teachers said I was cute. Within fifteen minutes of his obvious error in judgment, I had moved on. But from that day forward, the word ugly was subconsciously a part of my vocabulary.

Childhood is where genuine beauty lives, yet slowly, we forget it. Watch the confidence of a child around five years old. It is the age of innocence before the world interferes with telling them what they *should* look like. Before they understand how the rest of the world perceives beauty, *" 'Skinny' princesses with flawless skin are pretty"* and *"'chubby' princesses with any so called 'flaws' are ugly."* In time, playground crushes turn into cruel teenage heartache; middle school drama, physical changes, and intentionally defined images of beauty rip away their confidence.

An unsettling report from The National Association of Self Esteem showed that by middle school, 53% of American girls are "unhappy with their bodies." It grows to 78% percent by the time a girl reaches 17 years of age. Psychologist and professor Dr. Steven Hinshaw of the University of California at Berkley, has produced studies that have found that one in four girls fall into a clinical diagnosis of depression, eating disorders, cutting, or other mental and emotional disorders. They report being "constantly anxious, sleep-deprived, and under significant pressure to excel at 'girl skills,' achieve 'boy goals,' and be models of female perfection 100% of the time."

Middle school was when I started feeling immense pressure about my image. I started sneaking my grandmother's wrinkle creams at night because I thought the secret of her beauty lived in a magical jar of alpha-hydroxy lotion. Since my grandmother got numerous compliments on her skin in her late seventies, I was convinced she had discovered the fountain of youth. Fast forward one month later, my skin began badly drying out and my skin was so red I resembled a 'Flaming Hot Cheeto.'

Granny's magical potion was a little too aggressive for my young skin. Alpha hydroxy didn't make me any more beautiful —but it sure gave my grandma a merry laugh.

She told me, "Lisa, my 'little red crocodile,' the hope for youth is in that bottle, not beauty. Beauty is a whole different ball game. You're as pretty as you need to be."

UMMMMM. What? (rolls eyes as flakes of dry skin fall from my face) OOOKAAAAY GRANNY. I'm pretty sure my crush on the playground doesn't care what I carry within me. And what the hell does she mean, "Pretty as I need to be?!?" As a middle schooler, that's the same thing as telling someone, "Don't worry, you have a nice personality. Your looks will grow into it." Not what you want to hear in middle or high school when your mind runs on hormones and external validation.

I wouldn't understand what she meant by those wise words for many years to come because at that moment, at thirteen years young, my peers and the entertainment industry had already trained me that beauty was ONE HUNDRED PERCENT an image. I had to look like the most popular girl or whatever celebrity was trending at the time, and that image completely took over any interest in what I wanted to be when I grew up.

I went through so many phases of new images, like *grunge* and *pop star*. I permed my hair to look like the mega pop star Janet Jackson, only to end up looking like a human poodle. At one point, I had a cringe-worthy wave of super teased bangs that made me look like the youngest member of an eighties glam metal band. My image took a nosedive, and so did my grades— all of this in the name of "beauty." Then, oh God, the "sexy" look: short shorts and tank tops—or as my grandmother so lovingly called it, the Jezebel look—dominated my 15-year-old wardrobe! So many teenage girls looked like mini-adults at my school that the principal made a rule that your shorts and skirts had to reach your fingertips, and they banned heavy makeup.

Physical attractiveness is of overwhelming importance to us as we grow into our teens; it completely takes over all other forms of beauty and common sense. Completely living as an image to *fit in* is a frightening thought because this line of thinking distorts a healthy mindset for what it means to be a beautiful person.

Image becomes everything.

My best friend in middle school was obsessed with being skinny; she developed bulimia at 12 years old. Pretty scary. And now, with social media and photo filters informing girls and women of all ages how they will look if they are "flawless," it has become impossible for them to meet unrealistic standards of digital perfection. Subsequently, unnecessary plastic surgery procedures are continually on the rise.

One of the most influential developmental psychologists in his field, Erik Erikson, is famously known for *The Eight Stages of Psychosocial Development theory*. This theory states that personality development depends on resolving existential crises like trust, autonomy, guilt, intimacy, individuality, integrity, and identity from infancy to adulthood.

During each stage, a person experiences a psychosocial crisis that could positively or negatively affect their personality development. If the stage is handled well, a person will feel a sense of inner security and confidence. If the stage gets managed poorly, a person will emerge with a sense of inadequacy or low self-esteem.

While Erikson believed that each stage of psychosocial development was important, he placed added significance on stage five, the identity (or image) stage. The identity stage takes place from age twelve to eighteen years old, so middle and high school. Erikson described stage five as an ability to live by society's standards and expectations. At this age, we are discovering who we are. The opinions of parents, peers, social groups, and popular culture all start playing a role in shaping and forming our identity.

When parents are involved in their child's life praising academic achievements and genuine interest and making the perception of the teen's image a positive one, Erikson believes it sets the child up for a lifetime of confidence, independence, and a strong sense of self-identity. On the other hand, if a child gets raised in a verbally abusive home where they get constantly mocked for imperfections, like being overweight or developmental delays, are never praised for their strengths, and lack positive social networks, an internal conflict forms. A lack of self-identity and self-confidence sets them up for a lifetime of seeking outside validation because they are ill-equipped to generate it for themselves.

Every generation tends to do a good job ingraining the importance of academic achievement and looking good, but not the importance of teaching our youth what real beauty is. Often, parents deal with their own insecurities about aging and negative self-talk, which they picked up from their parents, who were taught that beauty is preserved for the young. Parents unconsciously reinforce that an external image is the most important part of one's identity. One of my favorite quotes on body image is by actress Kate Winslet. She said, "As a child, I never heard one woman say to me, 'I love my body.' Not my mother, my elder sister, my best friend. No one woman has ever said, 'I am so proud of my body.' That's very damaging because then you're programmed as a young woman to immediately scrutinize yourself and how you look." Winslet continued, "And so I stand in front of the mirror and say to Mia, 'We are so lucky that we've got a shape. We're so lucky we're curvy.

We're so lucky that we've got good bums.' And she'll say, 'Mommy, I know, thank God.' It's working, that thing that I've been doing. It's paying off."

A defining moment in my own life was when my cousins and I spent hours playing dress-up—I mean pageant makeup, Cinderella-style gowns, and our grandmothers' heels. We looked like we were about to go to a ball to win the admiration of a prince. We lined up and asked our grandfather, who was watering his garden, "Who is the most beautiful of all?"

He turned, smiled really big, and sprayed us all with the hose. We were soaked! He said, "Now you all look like wet dogs, so whichever one is the nicest."

That memory still makes me laugh because it taught my little, developing mind that I could spend hours adorning the outside to create a perfect image, which can so quickly be taken from me. And although I looked like a "wet dog," I was still beautiful because I was the nicest one of the bunch. (*Wink. Wink*).

I would often think back on that lesson when I worked in the cosmetic industry, as I encountered more and more teenagers and adults who felt worthless because they didn't fit an image, and sadly, an image was all they had to offer. Take, for example, Joan, a charming lady in her late fifties who visited a store where I was holding a promotional event. She was looking to buy new makeup because she was "heading back to Mexico to get the attention of a cabana boy." She had tried for years to get this man to date her seriously. She'd changed her look five years straight, beginning with something as simple as her hair, then escalating to more extreme measures like a nose job and breast enhancements. They always had fun together, but he never stuck around. But she was convinced this man would love her if she could figure out what he was attracted to. "Then," she said, "once I'm with him, I can slow down on the surgeries." Pretty crazy to think she couldn't break herself from this cycle after five years. It is rather obvious that this man was taking advantage of her misconception that image was all she had to offer. This conversation was a massive awakening. It isn't just young girls who seek attention with appearance, but grandmothers as well. It doesn't get easier with age. We are all disillusioned souls; if we think that if we could only be a little prettier, we would be accepted and live *beautifully ever after.*

Another harsh reality took hold when Linda, a more voluptuous woman in her mid-thirties, came in with her boyfriend, who consistently told her she was ugly and fat. She mentioned, when she was twenty pounds lighter, "He was a lot nicer." She was pleading with me to "make her pretty again." She was so focused on her image that she had a cosmetic magazine in her bag featuring the woman her man physically idealized. The picture looked NOTHING—I mean zero percent—like her! After speaking with her, I couldn't see how anyone could define this woman as an ugly person. She was so kind and spent her free time donating food to families in need. She was utterly lost in the idea that someone would love her if her image were "corrected" when all she needed was to change her mindset to one that would allow her first to love herself, then find someone who loved her for exactly who she was.

Many people might say, "What are you thinking?! 'Leave these men!" But like most addictions, breaking free is often easier said than done. The search for external validation runs deeper than most would like to admit. It's a mental stronghold consisting of low self-esteem that often gets seeded in childhood. And like some addictions, recovery is a multi-step process. In this woman's case, the first step is to determine why she believes this man's words are valid. Why does she think changing her image will change who she is as a whole? Until she resolves those questions for herself, she will not feel validated, and she will depend on others, like this man, to be her validation for feeling beautiful and worthy.

A SUPER-awakening moment I had was when Clair, a sixteen-year-old girl who had her first interview coming up, wanted "to look as flawless as possible." She came in with her birthday money to buy a SEVENTY DOLLAR foundation. Seventy dollars is a lot of money for an adult to spend on a foundation, much less a sixteen-year-old who doesn't even need it.

The young girl saw an overly filtered Instagram model promoting the foundation and thought it would make her look like the model—when in reality, this foundation would wreak havoc on her young skin. The ingredients were made for a more mature skin. I told her this. She bought it anyway. But can we blame her?

We are a visual society.

Rice University performed a study known as the "Beauty Premium," which predicted that you're more likely to get hired for a job if an interviewer finds you attractive. Further, the study claimed that good-looking people make about 12% more money than less appealing folks, citing that attractive real-estate brokers bring in more money than their less attractive peers. According to a published paper in *Social Science Quarterly*, the more attractive political candidates are, the more likely they are to get elected. No wonder the cosmetic world is a 532B dollar industry.

We instinctively know what we find beautiful outside of the image, but with these kinds of stats, no wonder so many of us hide who we are, hoping to please someone else's aesthetic pleasures, hoping it will lead to success. But what happens when we have success and an off-balance perception of self? A battle ensues between whom we think we should be and whom we are meant to be.

Sure, attractiveness will open doors. It is human nature, but superficial doors are not solid. According to the same "Beauty Premium" study, attractive people are expected to perform better than their less attractive counterparts. Similarly, when attractive people find themselves unable to meet the high expectations placed upon them, they may be hit with a 'beauty penalty.' In other words, they receive an initial advantage of some sort, but ultimately, they have to pay for it. A direct quote from the study: "You might see this as wages being depressed over time," says Rick K. Wilson, a Rice University political scientist who co-authored the study. "We have these really high expectations for attractive people. By golly, they don't often live up to our expectations."

We wreck ourselves to fit into a false image to please others. We mask our true identity and let our image speak for us. We know an attractive appearance will open doors, and we love the attention. Most clients I spoke with were not changing their image for themselves, but to capture the love or acceptance of someone else, get or keep a job, or look more flawless on their social media platforms.

They took jobs that didn't fit their personality or talents but fit an image society deemed "cool" and "sexy." Then, new, more attractive faces started showing up, so they had to keep spending more money to compete with an image because their talents didn't fit the actual work qualifications. With every new enhancement on the outside, the inside was pleading louder and louder for someone to notice them for "who they are." In a profession of image, coworkers defined them so much by their exterior no one could take who they were serious. This is why it is paramount to honor God's given beauty to you—what suits YOU!

If a facelift will authentically boost your self-love or give you the confidence to land your dream job, I say go for it. If, instead, you're going to those extremes to get the attention of someone on social media, or you believe it will lead you to a career you want for status—don't expect a happy ending. Look, we all want to be attractive and desired, but the obsession with being attractive to EVERYONE and desired by EVERYONE completely ignoring the real power of beauty is dangerous and pointless. All the cosmetic surgery in the world cannot achieve universal desirability anyway.

Social media is a double-edged sword.

The freedom of expression and social connectedness can be pretty satisfying, but the impact of lies and manipulation on underdeveloped minds is frightening. Generation after generation, we are being taught to compete with image, not with talent. The lies seduce us into believing that the more makeup we apply and the sexier we look, the fewer problems and challenges we will have.

Can you hide this big nose?

Can you make me tanner/lighter?

Will these lashes open my eyes?

Can you make me look like (Insert trending celebrity)?

Ugh, I'm so ugly!

Just fix me!

I saw this model in a magazine.

Personality is for fat people.

After years of hearing so much negative self-talk from customers in the industry, I was tired of the superficiality of it all. THINK BIGGER. Each of us is a gift to life. We have such a short time to make our impact, yet we waste it away on pleasing the eye of someone else. For me, the cosmetic and fashion industry just wasn't fun anymore. I had essentially become a therapist. How could I persuade these beautiful people to BE ATTRACTIVE, NOT DESPERATE? Enhancing is okay. Changing the whole person is not. It's just a fragile shell you are changing when in reality, the world needs who you are underneath that façade—the beautiful spark that only you can give. Altering your "big" thighs will not change your purpose. Too many people are getting concealed in a made-up world.

Look inside.

The school of life has taught us that to be beautiful is to be attractive. Imagine if people spent the same time perfecting the inside, the part that can't be taken away, as much as the outside, especially in our childhood and teenage years. Imagine if parents taught lessons like this in fun ways, lessons that teach children about the true nature of beauty. Art classes should be mandatory, and not instructed art, but art that leads us to trust our innate sense of beauty through free artistic expression using all five senses instead of the most popular one these days, the *sense of sight.*

Children and teenagers should be out of pageants and back into nature, reflecting on simple beauty. The world is filled with extreme wonderment and beauty. Immersing ourselves in simple beauty, like fully appreciating a sunset or sunrise helps us discover that we are a part of the beauty. We should spend those valuable childhood years providing productive ways that keep children asking questions, using all five senses, and without judgment. A child aware of what sights, sounds, and tastes are pleasing to them will naturally gravitate toward what they enjoy, discovering what talents and gifts they have. Parents should use extreme caution when considering entering their children and teenagers into pageants that display their faces and figures for judgment. While there may be some benefits and life lessons, the exposure to intense competition based on their image or appearance can irrevocably misshape their perceptions of the beauty that is distinct to each of us. Competition can send the message at such an early age; *your competitors' gifts are better than yours. Either find new talents or copy your competitors' talents.* Parents then risk turning their children into hyper-competitive adults who are never satisfied or insecure adults with self-esteem issues.

I understand that people hate clichés like, "Beauty is on the inside." And I can't blame them because we are hypocritical in our society. Cosmetic companies tell us to look on the inside all the time. They like to throw in slogans of self-positivity while handing us a jar of face cream without explaining how this will possibly help us "on the inside." What are we supposed to do, eat the face cream? It's absurd.

As an adult, the only way to age gracefully is to maintain a consistent practice of changing your own mind to believe the truth that you're attractive and worthy. The outside world will always have something to criticize. Criticism is good for business. But honey, sweetie, gorgeous girl—the outside world isn't with you every single day. But the people who genuinely love you see the beauty that radiates from inside. No one criticizes their parents for losing their youthful looks. We know it is part of life. But the cosmetic companies are telling you that your parents become less beautiful because they are old, that all your mom and dad have accomplished in life means nothing because they are no longer young and attractive.

Are fleeting thoughts from strangers worth a lifetime of insecurity? Is chasing an image worth losing the gifts you possess? No, it's not. Even the oldest book in the world, The Bible, expresses how placing too much value on the outside ruins the whole being. It makes it clear: identity is found in our actions, our character. Here are three of my favorite verses about image:

II Corinthians 4:16 "That's why we are not discouraged. No, even if outwardly we are wearing out, inwardly we are being renewed each and every day."

Psalm 139:14 "I praise you, for I am fearfully and wonderfully made. Wonderful are your works; my soul knows it very well."

Samuel 16:7 "But the Lord said to Samuel, "Do not look on his appearance or on the height of his stature, because I have rejected him. For the Lord sees not as man sees; man looks on the outward appearance, but the Lord looks on the heart."

CHAPTER TWO

WHAT IS REAL BEAUTY?

"If you're pretty, you're pretty, but the only way to be beautiful is to be loving. Otherwise, it's just congratulations about your face."
— *John Mayer*
(Singer, songwriter, and guitarist)

MERRIAM WEBSTER DEFINES BEAUTY AS:

"The quality or aggregate of qualities in a person or thing that gives pleasure to the senses or pleasurably exalts the mind or spirit."

The cosmetic industry defines it as the current trending celebrity, cause, or social media influencer who sells the most cosmetics.

"If you sense there must be more, there is more."
— Alan Cohen
(Businessman and author of 24 inspirational books)

Trying to define beauty is an arduous task. Philosophical debates on whether beauty is aesthetic or moral or subjective or objective have been going on for centuries. Aristotle (384-322 BC) defined beauty in metaphysics as having order, symmetry, and definiteness, which the mathematical sciences exhibit to a particular degree. David Hume (1711–1776) argued the opposite, saying, *"Beauty is no quality in things themselves: It exists merely in the mind which contemplates them, and each mind perceives a different beauty. One person may even perceive deformity, where another is sensible beauty, and every individual ought to acquiesce in his own sentiment without pretending to regulate those of others. To seek the real beauty, or real deformity is as fruitless an inquiry as to pretend to ascertain the real sweet or real bitter."*

I believe every one of us holds an essence or *spirit* about us that is our beauty, and that's why we can recognize it in another. We all have it. I also believe that for beauty to hold any special meaning, there must be a constant that we all hold true about it. Otherwise, it would be safe to say that garbage smelling of dirty diapers, surrounded by flies, is beautiful. I think we can all agree this isn't true. Beauty, then, must align with some set of conditions that cause you to sense that it is beautiful.

How do you describe beauty without words? You describe it in feeling! Beauty has an essence all its own, and it's unique to every individual and object we encounter. We sense whether someone is living in their beauty. We do not sense or feel their image. Image is tangibly seen. Beauty, therefore, is the special part of our essence or spirit.

The beauty within people can be likened to The Law of Conservation of Mass. We all learned it in chemistry 101: The exact amount of matter and energy exists before and after the change—none is created or destroyed. A substance's physical properties may change in a material change, but its chemical makeup does not. For example, when a liquid turns into a gas, you may think the liquid is disappearing, but it is only changing form. If you measured the gas, it would have the exact mass as the liquid. I see beauty this way. Think of your consistent unchanging chemical makeup as beauty. Your true self. The soul of who you are. It never changes; it is always good and beautiful. You may change physically on the outside, apply cosmetics, change your hairstyle, or age, but the same amount of beauty remains constant within you. Beauty is the self that transcends all that is physical, the part of you that is steady and true and endeavors to push forward and express its virtue. Beauty is ageless. This is why men and women well into their 80s and 90s can still be described as beautiful.

"Everything will line up perfectly when knowing and living the truth becomes more important than looking good."
— Alan Cohen

A caterpillar turns into a butterfly. An oyster turns irritants and dirt into a pearl. A diamond is born under extreme heat and pressure. Instinctively we know this to be excellent and beautiful. Even during times that we perceive as adversity, something beautiful is being birthed all from the constant of beauty that we hold.

This is where *beauty is on the inside* rings true. The cosmetic and fashion industries have over processed the word beauty so much that we forget it is unique to each of us. This unique and unchanging essence that we recognize as beauty changes us into the butterflies we are destined to be. We are all ultimately good and striving to become better.

We all have the capability of bringing beauty into this world, even in—most especially in—adversity.

We are all given this essence of good paired with the capability and opportunity to illuminate it to the world. Think of life as a piece of artwork that you paint with your actions. Your actions lead to your masterpiece, the unique beauty you bring into the world. Even if there is a war going inside of you, your beauty doesn't disappear. Instead, it girds you with strength, perhaps hidden, until you choose to reveal or express it.

"...and when all the wars are over, a butterfly will still be beautiful."
— *Ruskin Bond, Scenes from A Writer's Life*

Even the most physically attractive person in the world must use their essence of beauty to evolve. We cheapen the value of beauty when we profess it as merely a perfectly proportionate feature. One thing I know to be true about beauty: it is ageless. Living in beauty (your actual state) requires an extensive amount of intention. It begins with nurturing the whole being. Discover what makes you happy, take care of the body that houses beauty, and serve in areas that are authentic to your soul.

Egotistical living hides beauty. People will see you with their eyes, but they won't feel your essence. The ultimate form of beauty inspires, informs, nourishes, satisfies the soul, and touches the soul of others. The true essence of beauty is virtue in action. That's how you emit a light about you that others cannot only see but feel.

The soul of who you are is beautiful and is meant to be shared with the world.

Confident people let go of superficiality and focus on revealing beauty to the world. They release their essence. Absolutely—they still have fun playing dress-up! They use cosmetics to feel good and present the best version of physical beauty—not change their whole look to appease the world or create an image.

If you've discovered your beauty within, you will view cosmetics as a means of fun. Even if you choose to employ some cosmetic procedures, the essence of who you are will outshine it all! Look at American country singer Dolly Parton. She has cultivated her inner beauty so much that any cosmetic work she's had done pales in comparison. She genuinely has fun with cosmetics and her "country barbie" image. She created her entire persona as a business decision, a brand, so to speak, early in her career. And I'd say it has worked for her for that purpose. But inside—her true beauty has never changed. She is so kind and confident in who she is. Her inner beauty makes it undeniable who she is, an ageless and beautiful soul. She is living in *soul beauty*, and it graces and transforms everything she touches with a spark of "Dolly" We can sense it. She is a bright light in the world, helping others. She has funded scholarships, wildlife charities, hospitals, and a literacy program that has provided more than one hundred million books to children. And she has always been this way. Her beauty is more powerful than her image. Her image is simply the vehicle for her beauty.

"I'm just a backwoods Barbie in a push-up bra and heels. I might look artificial, but where it counts, I'm real."
— Dolly Parton

The ability to spot a beautiful person is not found in one's eyes but in how they make you FEEL in their presence. They're so much at peace with themselves that you feel good just being near them, regardless of how they look. These are the men and women we often see surrounded by others. They're the most popular person at the party. It's never because they are the most physically attractive person in the room. It's because they are unapologetically themselves; as such, they emit a light and vibration from within that others can't ignore. They're uniquely their own person. They bring something new, peaceful, authentic. For this reason, you don't see their beauty; you sense it. These people nurture a spirit of beauty.

Audrey Hepburn is an example of transcended beauty. She was one of the most sought-after actresses of her time, simply gorgeous. As she aged, she just became more beautiful. Her essence radiated once the veil of image fell. When I think of Audrey Hepburn, she ignites a pleasant feeling of beauty and sophistication. She was gorgeous, but it was her encouraging words and undeniable confidence that transcended into genuine beauty. In Ms. Hepburn's opinion, **"The most iconic quality you can offer the world is finding out who you really are."** She's right! Why hide when there is only one of you in the entire world? Your incomparable beauty is your superpower! It is pretty crazy to think that there will never be another type of beauty like yours in the whole universe.

Hepburn was gorgeous but also a woman of virtue, which made her iconic to everyone. Her inner character makes her immortally beautiful. She reminds us of what it is to be a beautiful person. After Hollywood, Hepburn became a Goodwill Ambassador for UNICEF. She dedicated the rest of her life to helping impoverished children in Africa, Asia, and Latin America by working in the field, nursing sick children, and spreading awareness of the conditions of these nations, all while remaining a stylish icon (image). Her beauty shone in the form of stylish and sophisticated compassion.

When asked for her beauty tips on aging gracefully, Hepburn would recite humorist Sam Levenson's essay on beauty, so frequently that it has been attributed to her.

'Time Tested Beauty Tips'
by Sam Levenson

"For attractive lips, speak words of kindness.
For lovely eyes, seek out the good in people.
For a slim figure, share your food with the hungry.
For beautiful hair, let a child run his or her fingers through it
once a day.
For poise, walk with the knowledge that you never walk alone.
People, even more than things, have to be restored, renewed,
revived, reclaimed, and redeemed; never throw out anyone.
Remember, if you ever need a helping hand, you'll find one at
the end of each of your arms. As you grow older, you will
discover that you have two hands, one for helping yourself, the
other for helping others.
The beauty of a woman is not in the clothes she wears, the

figure she carries, or the way she combs her hair. The beauty of
a woman must be seen from in her eyes because that is the
doorway to her heart, the place where love resides.
The beauty of a woman is not in a facial mode, but the true
beauty in a woman is reflected in her soul. It is the caring that
she lovingly gives and the passion that she shows."

I have witnessed this authentic form of beauty a few times in my life, and I strive to embody it. I wholeheartedly believe genuine beauty radiates from the soul. It is our soul that is beautiful, not our image. It is immortal; the beauty you bring into this world echoes in eternity. It lives on, generation to generation. We are all connected through the residual beauty of prior generations. Without the beauty created by others, we would not evolve. I love asking people, *"What beauty will you bring into the world today?"*

I want to end this chapter with one of my favorite Sufi parables that nails the true meaning of beauty. It's called Four Wives:

'Four Wives'
A Sufi Parable
(Author Unknown)

Once upon a time, there was a wealthy merchant who had four wives. He loved the fourth wife the most and adorned her with rich robes, treated her to delicacies, and bought her anything she wanted. He took great care of her and gave her nothing but the best.
He also loved the third wife very much. He was

very proud of her and always wanted to
show her off to his friends. However, the
merchant was in a state of constant fear that
she might run away with some other man.

He also loved his second wife. She was a very
considerate person, always patient, and in
fact, the merchant's confidante. Whenever
the merchant faced problems, he always
turned to his second wife. She would always
help him out and guide him through troubled
waters.

Now, the merchant's first wife was a very loyal
partner and had made substantial
contributions toward maintaining his wealth
and business, as well as managing the
household. However, the merchant did not
love his first wife. Although she loved him
deeply, he hardly took notice of her.

One day, the merchant fell ill. Before long, he
knew his death was imminent. He thought of
his luxurious life and told himself, "Now I
have four wives living with me. But when I
die, I will be alone. How lonely I will be!"

Thus, he asked the fourth wife, "I love you most.
I have endowed you with the finest clothing
and showered great care over you. Now that
I'm dying, will you follow me and keep me
company?"

"No way!" replied the fourth wife, and she
walked away without another word. Her
answer cut like a sharp knife right into the
merchant's heart.

The sad merchant then asked his third wife, "I

have loved you so much for all of my life. Now that I'm dying, will you follow me and keep me company?"

"No!" replied the third wife. "Life is so good here! I'm going to remarry when you die!" The merchant's heart sank and grew cold.

He then asked his second wife, "I always turned to you for help, and you've always helped me out. Now, I need your help again. When I die, will you follow me and keep me company?"

"I'm sorry, I can't help you out this time." replied the second wife. "At the very most, I can only send you to your grave."

Her answer came like a bolt of lightning and the sound of thunder, and the merchant was devastated.

In his despair, a voice called out. "I'll leave with you. I would follow you no matter where you go."

The merchant looked up, and there stood his first wife. She was so skinny, as though she suffered from malnutrition.

Grieved, the merchant said, "I should have taken much better care of you while I could have!"

You see, we all have four wives in our lives. Among our four wives, the fourth wife is our body. No matter how much time and effort we lavish on it to make it look good, it will leave us when we die.

Our third wife is our possessions, status, and wealth. When we die, they will all be left for others.

The second wife is our family and friends. No matter how

close they have been to us while we lived, once we die, the closest they can be to our physical body is at our graveside.

The first wife is, in fact, our own soul. She is genuine beauty, a part of us often neglected in our pursuit of material wealth and the pleasures of our flesh. She is the only true good that follows us wherever we go. We are the sole creator of our inner and outer worlds. Perhaps we should listen to the voice of the soul and nourish her now, rather than wait until we're on our deathbed to realize we have neglected the only thing that lasts.

CHAPTER THREE

FOCUSING ON YOUR BEAUTY

"Every human being is not one, but two. One is the person we have become through the journey of the past. The other is the dormant being of the future, who we become through our forward journey."
— *Claus Otto Scharmer*
(Senior lecturer at the Sloan School of Management, Massachusetts Institute of Technology)

I DO NOT BELIEVE GENERATIONS OF YOUR ANCESTORS LED TO the chance encounter of your parents, resulting in a unique being, just for you to strive to be or look like someone else. Actually, I'm certain of it.

Each of us is blessed with abilities and attributes that no one else in the world possesses. Of course, there are similarities, but no one will perform a task, look at an issue, or deal with the same situation in the same way.

"No DNA is the same. It's pretty crazy to think about. Human DNA is 99.9% identical from person to person. Although 0.1% difference doesn't sound like a lot, it actually represents millions of different locations within the genome where variation can occur, equating to a breathtakingly large number of potentially unique DNA sequences."
-Helix Genome Platform

Yep! That 0.1% is what makes you, YOU! Ignoring it is like tossing your best gift on Christmas morning. As Einstein pointed out, a fish isn't constructed for a tree. If that fish ignores his instincts and decides to climb a tree, he's working to perish. Even if he finds an oxygen tank and ends up climbing it, is he going to be happy with the birds who are simply going to eat him?

Ignoring our own passions and chasing the success or image of someone else is likened to a fish climbing a tree. It's not going to end well for anyone but the birds.

"No man ever yet became great by imitation."
— Samuel Johnson
(English writer who made lasting contributions to English literature as a poet, playwright, essayist, moralist, literary critic, biographer, editor, and lexicographer)

It's natural to admire someone else's success and their successful mannerisms, but only if it fits into your true identity and you truly make it your own.

Think of it like a musician who covers someone else's song but gives it their unique sound and flair. These brave artists are the musicians who ultimately get recognized, not the cover bands who record it identically to the superstar they're covering.

When I think of someone who achieved the success of others on her own, Cleopatra comes to mind. No matter what Hollywood says, Cleopatra wasn't conventionally pretty. Her nose was long and beaky, and she had double chins. Cleopatra did not strike Antony and Caesar to their knees with her good looks but rather with her fierce dynamism. She controlled her aura of beauty and understood fully what her endowments were. Cleopatra noticed the interest of those she craved in her life and shifted it into part of her appeal, but it continuously flowed naturally, never forced. She found a unique style of capturing attention. She knew her soulful strengths and used them to take over an empire.

The venerable writer Plutarch declared that Cleopatra's beauty was "not altogether incomparable" and that it was instead her "mellifluous speaking voice" and "irresistible charm" that made her so desirable. When you lead from the soul, people take notice.

If we are impure about who we are, we will never be content. If we waste our days neglecting our true identity and struggling to fit in when we are designed to stand out, we will become lost in the crowd. Authenticity is the path to triumph. I regret to report, but you will NEVER be permanently attractive to everyone, anyway. It's a waste of time, energy, and money to assume so. It's like actress Dita Von Teese said so eloquently, "You can be the ripest, juiciest peach in the world, and there's still going to be somebody who hates peaches."

An acorn would never grow into an oak tree if it didn't adhere to the laws of nature. Likewise, you will never fulfill your maximum potential if you continue following the latest social media trends, when in fact, the only way to beauty is living from the soul of who you already are.

"The soul has been given its own ears to hear things that the mind does not understand."
— *Rumi*
(The greatest Sufi mystic and poet in the Persian language)

A violin is pretty to look at, but it's the music that generates its beauty. As one of my favorite spiritual authors, Dr. Wayne Dyer, lovingly said, **"Don't die with your music still in you."** Real beauty encourages us to care more about becoming genuine versions of ourselves and never settling for less. We all have an instinct to produce something beautiful, to leave behind a warm remembrance for those we cherish. Think of friends and family you've lost. Their appearance is never the most significant memory left behind.

One of my favorite poets and civil rights activist, Maya Angelou, was spot on when she said, "I've learned that people will forget what you said, people will forget what you did, but people will never forget how you made them feel." The way you make someone feel in your presence is your legacy.

What I know to be true about life is that when we step out of ego and listen to our inner voice, when we use it with positive intent, to be of service to others, to make them feel good, the right individuals and opportunities "*magically*" appear.

The ego doesn't want to accept the soul's desire for service in a world where we get valued on appearance and materialism. So, we push that inner voice out because it makes us look "uncool" and "not sexy" enough. We spend our free time and thoughts making up new ways to impress others to give our egos strokes of accomplishment and acceptance. Years rush by, and one day we wake up and wonder, *where has all the time gone?* To hear the inner soul and truly experience a fulfilled existence, the ego needs to learn how to coexist with the soul. All successful men and women realize ego work is fulfilling only to an extent, right before it suddenly stops.

Ego Trip: An incredible journey to nowhere.
— Robert Half
(Co-founder of the world's first and largest accounting and finance staffing firm)

"Failure comes from ego, greed, envy, fear, and imitation. I have success, not because I am smart, but because I am rational."
— Warren Buffett
(The world's third-richest man with a reported net worth of $86 billion)

The soul's mission is always more extensive than the egos.

Spend some days doing only soulful activities, which put a smile on someone else's face and request nothing in return. Step outside of your head and hang out with the heart. Engage your faith with something greater than personal identity. I'm not talking about social rules and expectations or attending a couple of services at a church. I mean, really study faith, the faith that draws you away from ego. Ego quiets when you study the soul.

You can start by studying sacred literature about ancients, philosophers, emperors, monarchs, and saints and how they lived. You will see a pattern. The most respected individuals in history are motivated by their God-given talents; they are tuned in to the soul to see that which is meaningful. Empires have always been taken down by ego. The ego operates with limited beliefs and narrow thinking. It serves only itself. Given too significant a role, the ego drowns out our spiritual gifts, which we've been given to enrich the lives of others.

"As each has received a gift, use it to serve one another, as good stewards of God's varied grace."
I Peter 4:10

The latest science reports that true happiness comes from practicing compassion. When we realize we are all part of humanity, not separate, and we encourage our fellow man, that's when we feel most connected to the world and experience true meaning and purpose.

Research by post-doctoral researcher David Rand at Harvard University reveals that our first impulse is to help others. In another intriguing experiment out of Harvard, students' immune systems were elevated just by watching a video of Mother Teresa tending to the sick.

Professor of Medicine and Psychiatry and Biobehavioral Sciences, Steve Cole at the University of California at Los Angeles, and APS Fellow Barbara Fredrickson at the University of North Carolina at Chapel Hill performed a study on inflammation, the source of many diseases that shorten lifespans. They reported that people who were *very happy* because they lived a life of purpose or meaning serving others (also known as "eudaimonic happiness") had low inflammation levels. Those who were *very happy* but living just for themselves (also known as "hedonic happiness") were found to be stress-free and happy but still had high inflammation levels.

*"Everybody can be great because anybody can serve. You don't
have to have a college degree to serve. You don't have to make
your subject, and your verb agree to serve... You don't have to
know the second theory of thermodynamics in physics to serve.
You only need a heart full of grace, a soul generated by love."*
— *Martin Luther King*
*(Baptist minister and activist who became the most visible
spokesperson and leader in the American civil rights movement
from 1955 until his assassination in 1968.)*

———

In a 1951 radio show, host Edward R. Murrow asked the American audience to send their most strongly held beliefs in essays. He called the segment *'This I Believe.'* People from all walks of life wrote in, celebrities to the ordinary citizens. Mr. Murrow discovered that Americans share a set of common core beliefs in freedom, life, love, liberty, duty, honor, and country. No one mentioned *being the most attractive* or wanting to *fit into the crowd*. Murrow believed we all crave to serve in these areas, and we can, in diverse ways, that fit our individual talents. Here are Murrow's exact words:

*"I believe in my fellow citizens. Our headlines are splashed
with crime. Yet for every criminal, there are ten thousand
honest, decent, kindly men. If it were not so, no child would live
to grow up. Business could not go on from day to day. Decency
is not news. It is buried in the obituaries, but it is a force
stronger than crime."* — *Edward Murrow.*

Life is the appreciation of beauty while discovering that *you* are part of the beauty of life. That's why honoring your soul gift to the world is so necessary. The beauty within creates life. That message is expressed everywhere. Think about something as simple as a tree. Most people will walk right past it. However, I see a bird's home, oxygen, deep roots starting from an acorn, a story—each belonging to those who have passed the tree. Think of yourself as that tree. You may never know the kind of impact your purpose makes on those around you.

There is a verse in the Bible I love, Matthew 6:21: *"For where your treasure is, there your heart will be also."*

Passions are given to us for a reason. Follow them. They'll lead you to purpose and the feeling of genuine beauty.

> *"The best way to lengthen out our days is to walk steadily and with a purpose."*
> —*Charles Dickens*
> *(Regarded by many as the greatest novelist of the Victorian era)*

I feel most beautiful when I'm writing to others. I wrote uplifting poetry as a child, and I won a couple of book contests at school. Unfortunately, I didn't have the parental guidance I needed to pursue this passion. As a young person without discipline, I drifted.

Gratefully, that little voice never went away. And, though I frequently ignored her, I never stopped listening overall. And now here I am at 40-years-young, writing a book. Callings that serve others don't just go away; they keep nagging you. That inner *you* (your soul) knows that "the squeaky wheel gets the grease." It's incredible to me that my life choices led me back to writing. I'm so glad I never drowned out that voice completely.

You become your habits.

The spirit of beauty and purpose is available to everyone. If you can't hear your inner voice, experiment with activities until something clicks. A smile shows something has been sparked inside. Every morning wake up a little earlier, and before you start your day, do one thing that helps you accomplish your goal. Make sure it makes you healthier, more intelligent, or happier. Find a hobby that makes you forget about your troubles, like yoga, running, comedy, playing with makeup, singing, mathematics, writing, or meditation. Your primary focus should be to find out what sets your soul on fire.

"There is no time for cut-and-dried monotony. There is time for work. And time for love. That leaves no other time."
— Coco Chanel
(Fashion designer, founder of Chanel)

You are the greatest teacher you'll ever know. You only need to expand your worldview.

And watch out; there is a difference between a fantasy and a calling. Fantasy is a daydream, usually of something that validates the ego. As the ole wise saying goes, *"Confidence is a smile, Arrogance a smirk."* Callings, on the other hand, always help other people. Egocentric dreams are never completely fulfilling because they are materialistic. Ego actually destroys the dream. The dream is to know thyself and know thy beauty. Learn new things, gain wisdom, engage your faith, and serve one another. Are you smiling or smirking?

"I think everybody should get rich and famous and do everything they ever dreamed of so they can see that it's not the answer."
— *Jim Carrey*
(Actor, comedian, writer, producer)

Reality rarely lives up to fantasies. We all want to be acknowledged and appreciated, but not at a cost that destroys us and the essence of our beauty within. Egotistical goals ruin beauty. Take a long hard look at why your dream is your dream. Is it to please yourself and get rich to buy a new Rolls Royce? Is it to evoke people to say, "Oh wow, they are so wealthy and gorgeous?!" Or is it to discover the real magic and beauty life offers while helping others along the way? We are literally flying through space, on a rock, around the sun. If that doesn't make you take a step back and think, *wow, there must be more than being wealthy and gorgeous*; you're trapped in limited thinking.

Success, like knowledge, should be shared.

I want to stress that there is nothing wrong with seeking success or wanting to look great. Success is the only way to really help others. You need to nurture yourself first so you, in turn, can encourage others, both mentally and physically. Frankly, the world needs more humble and successful beauty— BUT, NEVER, EVER let your identity be wrapped in dollar signs or image. Once you become successful, "Send the elevator back down," meaning, be prepared to help those below you on the ladder so that they too can enjoy success.

It's getting harder every day to remain true to our inner voice with the bombardment of social media. As a culture, we are becoming more narcissistic and voraciously pursuing to enhance worldly ideas of ourselves. Everyone wants the most likes, to be the coolest, or the richest, the prettiest, and the list goes on.

A word about social media: it is a platform where we compare ourselves to unrealistic images and expectations. The images we see have been altered, filtered, and air-brushed 99% of the time. And there is no substance to those photos. Most people post for attention; they're crying out inside. They need likes and views to feel validated. All they want is to be noticed and adored.

It's a hard-fought effort to self-discovery. No one can do it for you. As much as I'd love for this book to solve all your problems, it won't. It's just a start, an inspiration. **DO THE WORK.** Be proactive. Start by noticing. You can't fix what you can't see. Ask family and friends to tell you gently where your weaknesses are. Constructive criticism is good. Pay attention to how things make you feel and why. Are you feeling like crap because of air-brushed girls you saw on social media and then compared yourself to them? Are you self-sabotaging and not even noticing it?

Ego tells you beauty is all about you, and maybe in a small way, it is because you can only bring *your* authentic beauty into the world. But are you using it for the agenda of the soul? Or to please onlookers? What is your real journey? Ask yourself:

1. Who am I? (You figure out who you are by first figuring out who you are not. What are you doing just for show?)

2. Why did my spirit take me here?

3. What do I intend to do?

4. Who am I spending my time with? This includes not only the people you share time with but the time you spend on entertainment. What are the shows you watch and the books you read filling your mind with? What you think, you become.

5. How can my strengths serve others?

You will never get to *Destination Beauty* without honestly acknowledging all of yourself and where you'd like to go outside of image. You may have lost who you are to a job, a bad relationship, to the needs of your kids, your health, or trauma, but believe me, you are still in there. All you have to do is remove your identity from the pain.

Some of us bury our authentic selves because we have been hurt or traumatized by the world. We put up a wall to protect our soul and live behind an image that pleases others because it is safer. No one asks too much of you when you glorify that all you are is an image. The truth about yourself, who you are hiding from the world, is more beautiful and will make you more successful than any image you believe will make you happy. It's so important to get back to your true self to live an authentic, beautiful life. You'll never find yourself in another person. If you're heading down that road, you're using someone else's map, marked with someone else's streets, their rugged territory, and their past. You'll eventually hit a roadblock because you can never become someone else 100%. Their map is useless to you. Follow your own map to *Destination Beauty*, which begins and ends with you. It starts with navigating and healing residual hurts that have you stuck on false beliefs about yourself.

CHAPTER FOUR

MAKE PEACE WITH YOUR PAST

"In the process of letting go, you will lose many things from the
past, but you will find yourself."
— Deepak Chopra
(Author, prominent figure in the New Age movement)

THE WORLD IS FULL OF SUBLIMINAL MESSAGES AND heartaches. Every day something is published or said that shapes the way we see ourselves. An unhealed mind easily gets manipulated into believing someone else's way is better. We can't escape suffering in this life. Pain will inevitably revisit us from time to time but allowing it to sabotage us to our very core, robbing us of our joy, and denying ourselves a life of beauty is the greatest tragedy any of us could face.

Buying into the lie that you are not appealing because of your past is a detrimental belief. The first step to recognizing who you are is to reject this misbelief. Uncontrolled trauma robs us of our beauty. It puts a veil of lies over our eyes that says we aren't good enough and clothes our spirit in worldly apparel. We become vulnerable, close our authentic selves, and shut people out because we expect to get hurt again. The soul desires to be revealed, to be known. The more we seal it off, the more fearful we become. Our fear may manifest itself as panic attacks, anxiety, and depression. Trauma not only kills internal beauty but destroys the external as well. Trauma puts our body in an endless loop of the fight-or-flight response, continuously releasing all kinds of beauty robbing chemicals into our physical bodies.

Psychodermatology is a relatively new field that addresses the impact of an individual's emotion as it relates to the skin. Amy Wechsler, MD, is one of very few physicians board-certified in both dermatology and psychiatry. She says, "Premature aging and adult acne are the two most common skin problems I see, and stress and exhaustion are often at the bottom of both." Healing trauma-causing stress can alleviate or even cure skin issues.

There is a saying, *"what is within is without,"* meaning whatever is going on inside will reveal itself on the outside. Many of us are all too familiar with the acne breakouts we get from too much stress. Let's further consider the visual impact of other emotions, such as "bottled up" anger. Anger affects our facial muscles. Anger has even been shown to decelerate the skin's healing process, increase the appearance of wrinkles, and produce dark spots on the skin's surface. Holding on to anger causes repeated frowning and furrowing of eyebrows. And jealousy—jealousy is probably the biggest thief of authentic beauty. Unmanaged jealousy, specifically for appearance, compels us to spend valuable days striving to become someone else, which is impossible to achieve. Our failure and striving can lead us down a spiral of unnecessary anger and depression. These emotions are not limited to expressions of overwhelming sadness, either. They can reveal themselves in the form of overindulgence, substance abuse, relationship problems, unnecessary plastic surgery, and anxiety.

"I've spent most of my life walking under that hovering cloud,
jealousy,
whose acid raindrops blurred my vision
and burned holes in my heart.
Once I learned to use the umbrella of confidence,
the skies cleared up for me
and the sunshine called joy became my faithful companion."
— Astrid Alauda
(Poet)

If we want to live in a beautiful state of mind, at some point in our lives, we must heal our hurts and turn the lessons from the past into something meaningful.

"I can bear any pain as long as it has meaning."
- Haruki Murakami
(International best-selling author of postmodern literature)

———————

A term has been coined by the University of North Carolina psychologists Richard Tedeschi and Lawrence Calhoun: "posttraumatic growth." It describes the surprising benefits many survivors discover in healing from a traumatic event. After counseling bereaved parents, cancer survivors, veterans, the grief-stricken, severely injured, and prisoners, researchers found growth in five main areas: personal strength, deeper relationships with others, new perspectives on life, appreciation of life, and spirituality.

The most impactful and beautiful stories are often those of

the underdog who overcomes obstacles that would have destroyed most. You can sense their strength, determination, and beauty, regardless of how they look on the outside. These people triumph through the storm and master the lies of the mind. They prove to us that who we are inside is more powerful than any of the chaos happening on the outside.

"The greatest glory in living lies not in never falling, but in rising every time we fall."
-Nelson Mandela
(One of the 20th century's most important civil-rights change-makers, Nelson Mandela, devoted his life—including 27 years in prison—to bring an end to the cruel segregationist policies of South Africa's apartheid system.)

Finding our hope amid chaos and releasing our anger to create positive change deepens and accentuates the beauty around us. Hope is why I love the arts so much. Some of the most beautiful pieces blossom from beneath the chaos. Quality art often has an emotion attached. Think of a classical piece of music like Wolfgang Amadeus Mozart's *Requiem in D minor*. Mozart started writing this beautiful piece in the midst of dying, and though he never finished, what he left behind can be *felt*. One can sense his darkness, anger, and fear turn into hope, light, and acceptance.

"As death [...] is the true goal of our existence, I have formed during the last few years such close relationships with this best and truest friend of mankind that death's image is not only no longer terrifying to me but is indeed very soothing and consoling."
— Mozart
(A prolific and influential composer of the Classical period)

"We're only lucky enough to see the wonders of nature's canyons because they're gracious enough to show us the places they've been damaged."
— Curtis Tyrone Jones
(Author of Guru in The Glass)

The start of my journey was predestined for doom. I should have a harsh view of the world in which beauty is a fairytale rather than a reality. I was born into what most would call a hideous world. There was never a dull moment. I saw far more than any child should, from living with family members who were drug users and alcoholics, witnessing domestic abuse, and mourning many tragic and early deaths.

I was orphaned at the age of three when I lost my mother, who was eight months pregnant, in a horrific car accident. The driver of our car lost control, and my mother was thrown through the windshield. My mother and unborn sibling died a few hours later. My mother was only twenty-three. My six-year-old half-sister and I were both in the car. Her left arm got completely cut open after being thrown out the back window. She still has scars. I was pushed to a floorboard, and by God's grace, we both survived. Soon after, my less than part-time father completely disappeared. He was living the "Rockstar" lifestyle and believed he was too young to have a child. So, my maternal grandparents adopted us.

Through the years, I watched my grandparents get plagued with countless tragedies. Shortly after they were healing from my mother's death, another of their daughters died from drug and alcohol addiction. They took in three more grandchildren to raise. Tragedies like these are what I grew up seeing, which causes me to live in constant awareness about the beauty of forgiveness and compassion. I sometimes wonder what would have happened if, instead, my grandparents had hardened their hearts. If anyone has the right to be angry at life, it is them. On the cusp of embarking on their retired years together, two of their daughters passed away in horrible deaths, and they were suddenly stuck raising five grandchildren.

Soon after they took all of us on, my grandmother suffered a heart attack and stroke. She healed. Then she received a call that her father was sick and needed a caretaker. For five years, my grandmother and grandfather lived in separate cities while my grandmother took care of her ailing father. My grandfather would visit her on the weekends. Through all of their tragedy, my grandparents NEVER lost their loving spirit or sense of humor. During my teenage years, my grandfather would put up funny and inspiring handwritten notes. One read, "NO DDSS," which stood for "No drugs, drinking, smoking, or sex." Another read, "Speed kills. In and out of the car." And my favorite, which I was lucky to get a copy of, said, "You are judged on integrity, intuition, courage, knowledge, understanding, counsel, worship, wisdom, and reverence."

I still, to this day, do not know how they did it, but I believe it had a lot to do with their faith and tapping into the purpose of who they are (beauty). Beauty always triumphed over the anger. I will never forget a conversation my grandfather and I had when I was fifteen years old. My grandfather was sitting on the couch with a book in his hand, looking as peaceful as a cat lying in the sun. I asked him how he kept from losing his mind, and he said:

"Lisa, one thing about life is, none of us stay on earth. Life is a school for the soul. We are here to learn and become better beings. Don't live like you're here forever, but learn the depths of compassion and love like you are. Learn how to overcome. This life is only one dimension of many. Trials, tests, heartaches —they're all part of soul growth. How I treat you and others in my darkest hours says a lot about how much my own soul has grown."

Though I didn't realize it at the time, this one conversation was my epiphany of beauty. Tapping into the most beautiful part of our being is expressed on the outside as powerful, loving, authenticity. An original inspired poem is etched in my mind. I wrote it for his eulogy in 2008. The reason it drives me absolutely CRAZY that beauty is used so carelessly is that I saw real beauty in my grandparents. I saw the undeniable characteristics of beauty. No one could ever tell me otherwise. When I hear beauty, I don't think of mascara or perfect teeth. Because of them, I look inward.

"Thank You"
Lisa D'Anna

I wish I could write a poem that would describe exactly what he means to me, but there are no such words to describe such a prodigy...... A man so brilliant with SO MUCH wisdom to share that he could discuss anything---religion, science, music, even famous love affairs...... He gave advice that was wise and straight-cut such as, KEEP YOUR EYES AND EARS OPEN AND YOUR MOUTH SHUT! ... And some of the best life lessons I learned from him, like always keep dreaming even when things look grim. And no matter what in life you're taught, always ask why and keep your freedom of thought ...... He said to always give a second chance, because how do you get to know a person with one glance.... He was never judgmental or one to criticize and if you were to look at the world through his generous, loving eyes, you would see a world of beauty, miracles, truth, and love....... a world as heavenly as above. I believe his exterior shined from his soul and cannot be defined by any words other than "pure" and "whole." As I write this, tears fill my eyes because I wasn't ready to say my goodbyes. He was my hero, my mentor, and my friend, my courage that keeps me standing tall. To this beautiful man, I call Grandpa... Thank You.

I buried many traumas from my childhood, and after the death of my grandfather, the bitterness would spill out in ways that always destroyed me or those dear to me. I didn't particularly appreciate making close relationships because they were going to leave anyway. I attached this notion to almost everyone I met.

My grandparents stressed the importance of not letting bitterness grow in the heart. Beauty is the good in all things. Protecting our innocence and beauty is probably the most harrowing journey in this lifetime. It is far too easy to let trauma and hardships harden our hearts and seed anger and bitterness. It took me years to forgive. *Proverbs 4:23 says, "Keep your heart with all vigilance, for from it flow the springs of life."* I feel blessed to have experienced this most rewarding form of beauty. No matter the hardship, my grandparents protected their hearts, and the beauty of who they were radiated from them. This is how I know genuine beauty exists. I have witnessed it. I have been the opposite of it. I have felt it. I strive to be it.

Too often, we become so wrapped up in an injustice that has been done to us that we can't enjoy the present. Beauty IS stability in an unstable world. It took my sister and me quite some time to understand that life isn't fair. Even so, we still have to live and learn from it and turn the tears of loss into a river of hope. I've learned that while suffering, beauty comforts us, whether it's the beauty of our inner strength or someone else's; in times of chaos, real beauty revels itself and restores us. We have all been blessed with this sanctuary of beauty.

"And the God of all grace, who called you to his eternal glory in Christ, after you have suffered a little while, will himself restore you and make you strong, firm, and steadfast."
1 Peter 5:10.

If it weren't for my grandparents' abundance of unconditional love and their faith, I don't know where I'd be—probably in foster care, separated from all of my family, strung out, lost, and reliant on drugs to numb the pain. I saw first-hand how compassion and character could turn harsh tragedies into a higher purpose. And I've seen how inner beauty—who we are inside—can save us if we are willing to find our inner strength.

At the end of my grandmother's life, she was battling Alzheimer's. Often Alzheimer's patients become angrier as the disease progresses. But thankfully, she never once had a change of character — nothing but love radiated from her presence. Even when she was well into her eighties, no one EVER described my grandmother as old. She indeed discovered genuine beauty. I was always told how joyful, childlike, and BEAUTIFUL she was. They wanted in on the secret. Her secret: "Don't let the light go out!"

We all have a light inside that lights our darkest hour, and we must *"never, never, never, let that flame of light be extinguished,"* as my grandmother said. Always reignite it and make it brighter. That light isn't just for us; our light may light another's way. My grandparents were right. Their light is still lighting my way.

To this day, I remember a hymn my grandmother sang to me as a child, and I still sing it almost every day.

> *This little light of mine, I'm gonna let it shine*
> *This little light of mine, I'm gonna let it shine*
> *This little light of mine, I'm gonna let it shine*
> *Let it shine, let it shine, let it shine*
>
> *The light that shines is the light of love*
> *Lights the darkness from above*
> *It shines on me, and it shines on you*
> *And shows what the power of love can do…*

If I was raised under different circumstances, I'm sure I would look different, and I'm confident I would define beauty differently, too. My grandparents went through far more than I could ever imagine. Their strength helped me battle my anxiety and hypochondria. I made a conscious choice not to allow my childhood trauma to destroy the beauty in my soul. My past made me better, not bitter. What a blessing to experience the growth of inner strength by using the force of beauty. I will not say it's easy because it most definitely is not. I've experienced much heartbreak, anger, personal loss, shame, embarrassment, and ultimately losing myself to where I am today. And I still have more to learn, but I know first-hand beauty is powerful. It changes the way you see and think about hardship and can save the very essence of who you are. I love neurolinguistic programming (changing the way the mind perceives things) so much, I got certified in it. I'm always working to discover a purpose in each situation; this ability alone allows us to overcome depression. You have to live—you might as well live with the power of beauty within and purpose.

For a moment, think about how much you will gain by healing. Go within. Think about who you are, all the nitty-gritty, the good and bad. All of the nitty-gritty is you! *This is what makes you beautiful.* Your journey is unique. There may be similarities in stories, but no one shares your journey, and believe it or not, the world needs your message, your light.

There isn't a "cure-all" for trauma. It will always be with you, but it does get better with a conscious effort to use the strength of beauty to turn the pain into purpose. As humans, our minds are always searching for meaning. The trauma reminds us that there will always be hurt in the world; we can add to it, learn from it, or be a source of comfort.

Imagine if you forgot that fire burns. We only know of beauty because ugliness exists. We have to face our trauma head-on to draw any type of lesson or meaning from it. Masking the trauma only exacerbates the problem.

For example, the oversupply of antidepressants isn't curing people. Many times, medications for treating symptoms of depression are prescribed without even attempting to understand the root cause of the depression. Medicine is a temporary solution. Understanding the cause of the problem can often pave the way for lasting treatment. Some people need to take it, but it shouldn't be the end-all. In his book, *The Body Keeps the Score*, Dr. van der Kolk, who did the first study ever on Prozac to treat Post Traumatic Stress Disorder, says Prozac will never cure depression.

"Drugs cannot cure trauma; they can only dampen its symptoms."

When a traumatic event happens to a person, they attempt to suppress their memories by shutting down the areas of the brain that transmit visceral feelings and emotions that accompany and define terror to protect themselves from hurtful past situations recurring again. Trauma victims can unintentionally prevent themselves from feeling fully alive in the present. As a result, the traumatic memory remains stuck in the patient's mind, "undigested and raw." (van der Kolk, p. 258).

Dr. van der Kolk has shown that yoga appears to be a more effective treatment for traumatized people than pharmacological interventions in many instances. He is a massive proponent of "Self-awareness Therapy" and "Eye Movement Desensitization and Reprocessing" (EMDR). EMDR was discovered unintentionally by Psychologist Francine Shapiro in 1987 when she observed that as her eyes moved rapidly, it "produced a dramatic relief from her distress" (van der Kolk, p. 253) EMDR combines exposure therapy with rapid eye movement. "Therapists ask their clients to hold the memories of anxiety-provoking stimuli—for example, the painful memories of a frightening accident—in their minds. While doing so, clients track the therapist's back-and-forth finger movements with their eyes." At least twenty positive controlled outcome studies have been done on EMDR therapy. According to the EMDR Institute, which hosts a comprehensive list of EMDR-related research, some studies show that 84%-90% of single-trauma victims no longer have post-traumatic stress disorder after only three 90-minute sessions. Another study, funded by the HMO Kaiser Permanente, found that 100% of the single-trauma victims and 77% of multiple trauma victims no longer were diagnosed with PTSD after only six, 50-minute sessions. If you suffer from any type of trauma, I highly recommend reading Dr. van der Kolk's book. It's a powerful book on understanding the effects of trauma and offers various treatment alternatives to pharmaceuticals.

If you are not ready to see a specialist in your journey, I highly suggest the self-therapy practice of journaling, studying neurolinguistic programming, and prayer. The point of it all is to release suppressed feelings that are causing an imbalance in oneself blocking your beauty.

Journaling is an excellent vehicle for healing. An effective journaling exercise is to set a timer for five minutes and write whatever comes to mind. DO NOT put your pen down. If you have to write, *I don't know what to write* until something pops into your head, do that. So much can come from this exercise. Words are powerful and healing. Some topics to free write are:

How do I feel today?

Why am I hurt?

How can I heal my pain?

Why I think I can't heal.

The moment I changed.

When did I lose my innocence?

I am thankful for:

I feel happy when:

I am most afraid of:

What is beauty?

Why don't I feel beautiful?

Journaling is a great way to build confidence. The more we write, the more we explore thoughts we may not have known were lingering in the backs of our minds. It's a time to release negative self-talk and listen to your encouraging inner voice. She knows a lot!

Find groups online and friends who understand you, people who help you remember who you are outside of image. Frequent reminders of your strengths sustain confidence. I write down any compliment that is not focused on appearance, and when I don't feel my best, I'll go back and read them.

There are so many therapies you can try. But to truly become your most beautiful self, healing from past trauma is a must. You can't cover a hurt with makeup. The energy still envelopes you. You must learn to nurture yourself mentally, physically, and spiritually. Stop neglecting that little voice inside of you. You will never understand what you can learn from your trauma if you don't face it. I want to end this chapter with a parable I think of whenever I look back or start thinking, *"Why me?"* It is called *"The Story of a King and his Servant."* It always makes me feel a little less distressed. It may help you too.

'The Story of a King and his Servant'

(Author Unknown)

A king had a male servant who, in all
   circumstances, always said to him, "My
   king, do not be discouraged because
   everything God does is perfect. He makes no
   mistakes."
One day, they went hunting, and a wild animal
   attacked the king. The servant killed the
   animal but couldn't prevent his majesty from
   losing a finger. Furious and with no show of
   gratitude, the king said, "If God were good, I
   would not have been attacked and lost one
   finger."
The servant replied, "Despite all these things, I
   can only tell you that God is good, and
   everything He does is perfect. He is never
   wrong."
Outraged by the response, the king ordered the
   arrest of his servant. While being taken to
   prison, he told the king again, "God is good
   and perfect."
Another day, the king left alone on another hunt
   and was captured by savages who use human
   beings for sacrifice. While the king was on
   the altar, the savages found out that he was
   missing one finger. He was released because
   he was considered an incomplete offering to
   the gods.
On his return to the palace, he ordered the
   release of his servant and said, "My friend,
   God was really good to me. I was almost
   killed, but for the lack of a single finger, I

was let go. But I have a question. If God is so good, why did He allow me to put you in prison?"

His servant replied, "My king if I had not been put in prison, I would have gone with you. And I most certainly would have been sacrificed because I have no missing finger. Everything God does is perfect. He is never wrong."

Often, we complain about life and the negative things that happen to us, forgetting that everything happens for us.

We will never have the answer to why an incident was good or bad. Only God can be the real judge of that, but we can carry faith that someday we may understand why. Until then, we have to walk with the knowledge that life in itself is magical, and it's a blessing that we are even here.

CAPTER FIVE

I AM

"Be careful how you talk to yourself because you are listening."
— Lisa M. Hayes
(Author, relationship strategist)

WHEN WE DON'T REBUILD OUR BELIEF SYSTEM, WE INVEST SO much of our time listening to the voice of negativity. It is a waste of our valuable days. Negative thinking creates much unnecessary stress. Not one person is born into this world believing they are unattractive or inadequate. The lie starts when we experience rejection or trauma for the first time. Rejection and trauma scar us, teaching us that we must try harder for the approval of others, and we train ourselves to conceal our true selves (our genuine beauty) to fit in. We stop listening to the voice in our hearts and start listening to the voice in our head one-hundred percent of the time. Whenever I hear demeaning *I AMs*, like *I am worthless, I am so ugly,* or

I *am not qualified,* I associate it with unhealed trauma, hurt, comparison, or rejection.

Negative thoughts tend to turn into suppressed anger and envy, which are the complete opposite of beauty. Learn to let go of any emotion that's killing your beautiful spirit. As actor Malachy McCourt once said, "Resentment is like taking poison and waiting for the other person to die." The only thing we have control over is the present moment and our thoughts. I want to mention quickly, anger is okay as long as you use the anger as information and don't suppress it. Anger shows us what we're passionate about changing, and if we redirect that anger into a productive fight against injustices, we can bring beauty into the darkness. Suppressed anger does the opposite. The energy of suppressed anger builds and only makes you and your life more unattractive to the outside world. See your anger as information from your inner self, shining a light on areas that need healing in your life or the world. Expressed emotions are healthy. The only way to win at the game of life is to follow feelings into productivity and not destruction.

"Can you remember who you were before the world told you who you should be?"
— Charles Bukowski
(Poet, novelist, short story writer)

The frightening part of negative self-talk is that the lines we repeat to ourselves daily manifest themselves on the outside. Negative thinking about our bodies and image only creates more aging.

The mind and body have a powerful partnership. A minor example of this connection is an embarrassment. When we get embarrassed, we turn red, sweat, and maybe even shake. Internal thoughts trigger these physical reactions. When we are angry, our whole face scrunches up. You know this because you can see and sense when someone is angry or sad. Every reaction starts with a thought. Negative thoughts create a stress response in the body that begins changing us from the inside out. Ask any dermatologist what two factors speed up aging. They will tell you, sun and stress. A little scary but straightforward exercise is to put on a fitness watch and observe your heart rate increase or decrease with your thoughts!

New York City dermatologist Neal Schultz, M.D. notes in an interview with *Shape* magazine, "When your body senses something sad or stressful, your adrenal glands secrete hormones, including cortisol, epinephrine (known as adrenaline), and small amounts of testosterone, which trigger a cascade of reactions that can lead to excess oil production, decreased immunity (which can spur cold sores and psoriasis), and increased blood in your vessels (which can cause under-eye circles and puffiness)." Stress releases inflammatory mediators, which produce collagenase and metalloproteinases. These are the enzymes responsible for collagen and elastin breakdown leading to increased wrinkling, laxity, and aging.

Research out of Yale University shows depression can change a person's brain, hastening an aging effect that might leave them more susceptible to illnesses associated with old age. Researchers and scientists led by Laura Han from the Amsterdam University Medical Center in the Netherlands studied the DNA structure of people with depression. They discovered that the DNA of people with significant depression had aged an additional eight months on average than that of people who do not suffer from depression.

I AMs are the words used to instruct our brains on thinking, believing, and feeling. We hold these beliefs in the back of our subconscious. Long after we forget about them, the thoughts turn into symptoms such as fatigue, anxiety, weight gain, and depression.

"As someone thinks within himself, so he is."
-Proverbs 23:7

Once the effects show up on the outside, we get even more depressed. We try to ease pain and insecurity with outside means:

- Scrolling online to find a better life.
- Reading image magazines.
- Chasing the latest trends.
- Undergoing unnecessary cosmetic procedures.

Please let me emphasize, before considering any type of face altering procedure, check-in with your *I AMs*. What are they saying to you? If it sounds like, *"I am so ugly... I wish I were someone else..."* rather than something like, *"I am confident. I look pretty good, but I could use a small tweak,"* then please take a moment to reconsider. When you are an insecure person, even a "tweak" will not bring comfort.

Plastic surgeons change the outer beliefs, not the inner beliefs. Too often, an unhealed mind becomes obsessed with the idea that changing the outside or transforming oneself into someone else's definition of beauty will help them achieve personal happiness. Instead, it creates more confusion within the self. Several patients come out of procedures feeling worse and even more cynical and depressed. With a bit of research, you can find quite a few published studies from dermatological and psychological journals that support the theory that people who choose to have major unnecessary procedures, especially more than once, have some type of mental disorder like body dysmorphia. Body dysmorphia is a firm belief that you have a defect in your appearance that makes you so unattractive you need to "fix it" when, in reality, no one even notices the flaw you are fixated on. Self-criticism and inner beliefs take over. The individual retrains their thinking to internalize that it's their "flaw" that makes them feel that way when in reality, it's their own line of thought.

Neuroscientists have shown that 95% of our brain activity takes place on a subconscious level. It sounds crazy, but it's true! Only 5% of our cognitive activity (decisions, emotions, actions, behavior) comes from our conscious mind. The inner conversations we have with ourselves day in and day out are the most important because even after we forget about them, the brain does not. Dr. Emanuel Donchin, Director of the Laboratory for Cognitive Psychophysiology at the University of South Florida, stated, "An enormous portion of cognitive activity is non-conscious, figuratively speaking, it could be 99 percent; we probably will never know precisely how much outside awareness is."

The brain doesn't separate negative and positive thoughts. The ability to manage our thoughts is fundamental to our well-being. Every thought carries an energy that tells the brain which chemicals to release. When we have positive thoughts, we release *happiness* chemicals: *endorphins, serotonin, dopamine, oxytocin.* When we get stressed or think negatively, we release *fight-or-flight* chemicals like *cortisol.* Some cortisol is good for you. For example, if a wild animal is chasing you, cortisol levels enhance your ability to think quickly and run faster, but too much will wreak havoc on the outside. Neither our brain nor our bodies were intended to operate daily at these emergency levels. When the body releases stress hormones daily, we see the results in weight gain, heart disease, high blood pressure, and other outside signs.

Longevity is the brain's ability to adapt to ever-changing environments. The brain works to fulfill your thoughts. How we use *I AMs* is vital to controlling our lifestyle. The brain listens to the *I AMs* and not only sends out chemical responses but seeks people and experiences to validate those thoughts.

"The state of your life is nothing more than a reflection of the state of your mind."
-Dr. Wayne Dyer

Science is proving every day just how powerful our thoughts are. A functional MRI study of music-academy students contained two groups of beginning pianists. One group sat in front of the piano and visualized playing a sequence, while the other practiced it simultaneously. When they mapped the subjects' brains, scientists discovered that just doing mental practice resulted in the same physical changes in the visualization group's motor systems as the ones who physically practiced. The non-playing students had almost the same skills. To our brains, imagining doing something and actually doing it is interpreted very similarly.

Another study from Dr. Brian Clark, Ph.D. at Ohio University, shows that sitting still just thinking about exercise might strengthen us. Clark and colleagues recruited 29 volunteers and wrapped their wrists in surgical casts for an entire month. During this month, half of the volunteers thought about exercising their immobilized wrists. For 11 minutes a day, five days a week, they sat still and focused their entire mental effort on pretending to flex their muscles. When the casts were removed, the volunteers who performed the mental exercises had wrist muscles that were two times stronger than those that had done nothing at all. **Every tiny cell in our body is cognizant of our thoughts, feelings, and beliefs.**

"Mind is the Master power that molds and makes, And Man is Mind, and evermore he takes The tool of Thought, and, shaping what he wills, Brings forth a thousand joys, a thousand ills:— He thinks in secret, and it comes to pass: Environment is but his looking-glass." *James Allen*
(Philosopher and author of 'As A Man Thinketh')

The power and influence of thought are remarkable. I challenge you for an entire day, write down every moment a negative, *I AM* pop-ups. Awareness is key to changing your thoughts. Read back to what you are saying to yourself in your mind. Acknowledge that this is where you'll need to adjust your thinking. The goal is to get rid of the negative self-image you trained yourself to believe. REMEMBER, your *I AM-ness*, your consciousness, is how you change your world and bring out the dormant qualities within you. Acknowledging existing false beliefs gives you a starting point to correct these judgments. Awareness helps you recognize just how much the past forms your current beliefs— and a lot of them are FALSE. Unquestioning your thoughts are like leaving thieves and liars alone in your home to rob you of your beautiful treasures.

Most of us ignore, or worse, fight, these negative thoughts. Instead, acknowledge the thoughts and let them flow. Allow yourself to experience the physical and emotional feelings that come with the thought. *You can't fix what you can't see.*

Let's say you find yourself thinking; I'm *so unattractive, I'm going to be alone forever.* This very thought scares you, so you suppress it. Now, it's stored in the subconscious, where the subconscious will look for all the reasons you are unattractive and will be alone, only creating more emotional and physical stress. If you acknowledge that you feel that way, and talk to yourself with compassion, as you would a good friend, and you tell yourself that you're going to take effective action, so this doesn't happen, the subconscious will start showing you reasons why the negative thoughts are not true. Arguing or struggling to drown out or force unhelpful thoughts away only intensifies them and makes negative feelings worse. We all know how to *avoid the elephant* in the room, also known as the *"ironic process theory,"* whereby deliberate attempts to suppress specific thoughts make them more likely to surface. The elephants don't go away until we acknowledge their presence.

To change a thinking pattern:

1. Recognize that you have damaging ones.
2. Be aware of what you're telling yourself.
3. Introduce beliefs about yourself that you want to see.
4. Make it a daily habit.
5. If needed, see a therapist or seek one of the therapies mentioned in the previous chapter.

The change will not happen overnight. It is a lifestyle choice that requires commitment, but don't worry! It gets more manageable, and your life will only get better.

A super simple way to begin is to write positive *I AMs* on sticky notes and place those that resonate with you the most throughout your home. It's subtle and may even seem comical if you're in a dire situation, but it is a starting point and plants a tiny seed to reshape the subconscious. You are with yourself twenty-four hours a day, so make sure your environment and thoughts inspire you.

Words are powerful. I am obsessed with reading material about reshaping the mind. I study it a lot. Positive affirmations are mentioned in almost every book about the mind and thought-life. This isn't a coincidence.

I am not a person who tends to say positive affirmations aloud, especially when I'm in a negative situation. But I believe in reading and writing them down daily. I highly recommend writing exercises.

Here is an idea. Make a list for:

I AM BEAUTY

I AM HAPPY

I AM FIT AND HEALTHY

I AM BRILLANT

Each time you notice something that makes you feel that way, write it under the corresponding column. The subconscious will store them. Positive affirmations work so well because they activate the reward part of our brain (releasing those happy hormones). These are the same reward centers that respond to experiences that make us joyful, such as hearing our favorite song, seeing a favorite loved one, or going to a favorite restaurant. The reward center of the brain is so powerful that activating it has been proven to decrease pain.

Science is proving to us every day the power of our

thoughts. What you are focusing on becomes a reality. ***To think is to create.*** Every single thing in the entire universe started with a thought.

When you heal the mind and start focusing on the magic of everyday life, it doesn't just benefit our external world; we become more creative. We see potential where others see flaws. We realize everything holds beauty and a bigger purpose.

"Be Curious; Not Judgmental"
- Walt Whitman
(One of the most influential poets in the American canon, often called the "father of free verse")

If Swiss engineer George de Mestral didn't have an unbounding curiosity about nature and never looked under a microscope at the burrs that stuck to him after his walks in the woods, we wouldn't have Velcro. If people only saw nature as a nuisance, we may never have the field of biomimicry, which is devoted to imitating nature to solve human problems.

"Everything has beauty (purpose), but not everyone sees it."
– Confucius
(Philosopher, teacher)

Changing the way you see and think about yourself should be a number one priority. Remember, you are here to make an impact, not to collect other people's opinions that you are the most attractive person on the earth. Our external attractiveness is merely a bonus. Taking care of it is important because it is the *house of beauty*. The more beauty that resides inside of us, the more attractiveness will be revealed on the outside.

Motivational speaker and author Hal Elrod nailed it when he said, "Our outer world will always reflect our inner world. Our level of success is always going to parallel our level of personal development. Until we dedicate time each day to developing ourselves into the person we need to be to create the life we want. Success is always going to be a struggle to attain."

We all have a mission in this life. No one person is better, just different. The moment you accept this is the moment you start truly living. **YOU ARE ENOUGH.** Spend a week away from social media and magazines. When you look at something, be aware of how it makes you feel. Surround yourself with people and places that make you feel good as frequently as possible. And be that person to others. Practice getting in touch with your mind with techniques like meditation and check-in with yourself regarding your personal *I AMs*.

"Your best mirror is someone more beautiful than you."
— Chinese Proverb

You will know if you are evolving by looking at someone you find more beautiful or successful than you and appreciating their beauty and success without diminishing your own.

CHAPTER SIX

CONTROL YOUR ENVIRONMENT

*"The reasonable man adapts himself to the world: the
unreasonable one persists in trying to adapt the world to
himself. Therefore, all progress depends on the unreasonable
man."*
— *George Bernard Shaw*
(playwright, critic, polemicist, political activist)

IN THE LATE 1980S, TALK SHOW HOST DAVID LETTERMAN
stumbled onto a fascinating notion that room temperature
impacts the amount of laughter in the room. Letterman experi-
mented with the thermostat setting before his shows. The thermostat was set at 75 degrees, at 68, 65, and 71. At one taping,
he put it to 55, and the crowd reacted by laughing more than
ever before. Letterman didn't think he was amusing that
evening and credited the significant increase in laughter to the
temperature. From that point forward, every single taping
of *Late Night with David Letterman* was recorded in a 55-
degree studio in an attempt to increase laughter.

Some of us are under the notion that we have entire command over how our environment shapes us, that it is fixed, and we can't be influenced. This is far from the truth. Like Letterman's experiments, subtle tricks are practiced ALL THE TIME to evoke a controlled environment response.

Retail stores spend millions and millions on constructing environments which influence how much their targeted customer will spend. From the colors they use to the music they play to the lighting they arrange—all in hopes of seducing a buyer's senses. Playing slower or sentimental songs that are relaxing encourages lingering in stores longer. Fast music produces the opposite effect. Therefore, restaurants will play faster music, hoping to speed up your heart rate so that you will eat faster, and they can get someone else in your seat who will then do the same. Some fast-food restaurants use uncomfortable seats intentionally to generate customer turnover. The smell of cinnamon entices us to buy, which is why candle and home stores commonly choose that scent. These are only small tools retailers employ. I studied hundreds more in retail marketing courses, so much so that I could write a book on the marketing tricks alone.

Online environments are just as dangerous. For example, click on any site advertising a product that focuses on improving the image. Let's say you are researching a stationary bike to do spin classes at home. One search of that bike is going to bring up every man and woman on the internet with a body so toned; you'll start wondering if you searched for a stationary bike for 'Superman.' The ads are intentionally designed to make you feel insecure and ask, *why should I stop at only wanting to get healthy? I should probably buy the weight machines and trillions of supplements because that is the only way to turn my body into something better than what it currently is.* Most of the time, we don't think about it, but little pieces of negativity flow into our subconscious from suggestive advertising.

The advertising on social media targets us from our search history and the pages we follow. Cosmetic companies especially LOVE that you follow a thousand brands and celebrities. It makes it much easier for them to sell you the illusion that you can have it better, be better, look better.

Emergency Alert:
Replace image scrolling with productive scrolling. You'll get different ads and more productive content.

Where do you devote most of your time online: comparison or productivity? There is so much rich knowledge and information available online, from business or art classes to self-esteem courses, from writing a book to learning about the universe itself. It would be a mistake not to use the free online resources to increase your knowledge versus demeaning yourself in comparison.

"The only person you should try to be better than is the person
you were yesterday."
— Tony Robbins
(Author, coach, speaker, and philanthropist)

Remember, the subconscious makes most decisions. It is the advertising to your subconscious that is sneaky—and it works!

Big box cosmetic and department stores have nailed the *I look old; therefore, I am unattractive,* feeling most of us entertain our subconscious minds. Consider all the symbolism of youth throughout brick and mortar stores, the array of cosmetic selections, and the makeup artist standing up front, ready to show you how you can look younger, prettier, and trendier—NOW.

Their strategies compel us to lose touch with ourselves in an environment that is purposefully created to accommodate and comfort negative self-talk. Then, attentive salespeople with products disguised as healing and compassion—knowing darn well their company spent millions to make you feel like crap first—peddle a $500.00 "miracle" night crème into your hands and out the door.

As you move about your day, be mindful of how your emotions change in different atmospheres. Every environment maintains energy you will feel. We generally describe energy as something esoteric, but energy is how emotions and environments make us feel and the feeling we transmit to others.

How you feel at home is the most essential part of the day. Outside of work, home is where you spend most of your life. Make sure when you step into the house, there is someplace you can unravel and be yourself, a place to remind you that you are beautiful, that beauty is all around you, not just in the mirror. For example, I buy or pick fresh flowers every week. I keep photographs of my grandparents, daughter, husband, and a poem of Saint Francis placed where I will see them every day. They are constant reminders of what is *important or absolute beauty.*

"If you want to know the secrets of the Universe, think in terms of energy, frequency, and vibration."
— Nikola Tesla
(Inventor, electrical engineer, mechanical engineer, and futurist)

The fantastic news is, if you feel lousy in an environment, you can transform its energy. If a room has a negative vibe when you walk in, try opening a window to let in the fresh air. Redecorate a space with positive images. And I strongly recommend surrounding yourself with plants and flowers, as they carry their own uplifting life-giving energy. Roses and lilies are my choices. Together they can make a room smell like you're walking into a garden. The energy around roses vibrates at a super-high frequency of 320Hz, a healing vibration in plant medicine.

It has been demonstrated that when plants are placed in hospital recovery rooms or patients have a window to a garden that they heal sooner. Studies also show that plants in offices tend to decrease the rate at which employees are out sick. The effects of beautifying our indoor environment with plants are soothing and contribute to overall well-being. Indoor air quality is also better because of plants' ability to pull in stale air and breath out pure oxygen.

You may choose to repaint a room to give it a calmer, happier feeling. Multiple studies have shown that color can influence behavior and mood. Warmer colors increase arousal. Biologically, adrenaline begins to flow, blood pressure increases, and people perceive the temperature as warmer. They also experience high levels of stimulation. This is referred to as an *"arousal reaction"* to the ability of a color to activate biological triggers. While our perceptions of different colors are generally personal, there is a universal effect on emotions and behavior with warmer and cooler colors. It is possible to predict how most individuals will respond to color.

We often associate green with nature and growth because most people are around trees and grass and have witnessed plants growing. Blue is essentially universally calming because it's linked with elements like the sky and water. Allow as much light into a room as possible. It is correlated with a livelier frame of mind, enhanced morale, increased energy, and decreased eye strain. If you don't have a window or natural sunlight, get yourself a sun lamp (also called a SAD lamp ironically) or a light therapy box (a special light that mimics natural outdoor light). Light therapy is an impressive therapy for seasonal affective disorder.

"Have nothing in your home that you don't know to be useful or believe to be beautiful."
— William Morris
(British textile designer, poet, novelist, translator, socialist activist)

If you crave a beautiful life, it is up to you to establish one. Go around your home and take notice of how objects make you feel. All objects hold energy. Look at various objects that surround you and ask yourself, *Is this beautiful?* Try on clothes. How do you feel about wearing them? Any adverse reactions or thoughts at all? Throw it out! Holding on to anything that causes you to feel insecure, or triggers a remembrance of something painful, creates a merry-go-round of negative thoughts.

I am the queen of disorganization. Still, the objects that

surround me carry my mind to a beautiful place. There is a method to my madness. It's a constant routine. Growing up in a tumultuous situation with a lot of unpleasantness, I realized very early how necessary space is. When I was around ten years old, I found a spot in my yard filled with trees. I created a safe space where I would do things I enjoyed, like reading my favorite books or collecting beautiful rocks and leaves from outside. I would remain there for hours to distance myself from the chaos that surrounded me. We all need that space. No matter how youthful or mature we may be.

Our environment not only influences every single decision we make, but it changes throughout the day. You're in a different atmosphere at work than you are at home, or the gym, or at a coffee shop. Awareness of your environment will help you avoid places that make you feel unsettled or uncertain. For instance, when I walk into a dark, confined, or dirty space, I immediately feel a coldness, a sense of detachment, and increased anxiety. On the other hand, an open, flowing, well-lit area lifts my mood and reinforces whatever is most hopeful within me while I am there. The composition and decoration of a room can alter one's entire mood. In prisons, some chambers are painted pink to calm aggression. Often inmates themselves hang photographs of their loved ones and cherished letters from their family to soothe themselves.

Offer yourself a sanctuary of beauty separate from the unpleasantness of the world, even if it's outside of the home. For many people, nature is their only serenity. Find somewhere when it's possible to view a sunrise or sunset in the evening or morning. Beautiful moments affect our mood, thoughts, and days and, subsequently, create beauty in our world.

Being in nature possesses its own benefits. In a study of 20,000 individuals, a team led by Matthew White of the European Centre for Environment & Human Health at the

University of Exeter observed that *"people who devoted two hours a week in green spaces—local parks or other natural environments, either all at once or spaced over several visits—were more likely to report good health and psychological well-being than those who don't."*

Getting out of a negative situation into something more beautiful reminds our subconscious mind that there is a better way to live than the usual hustle and bustle of life.

I also recommend hanging visual boards where you spend the most time. Visual boards are a reminder to the subconscious of your ambitions and how you perceive your future. They are not just for arts and crafts—they stimulate motivation and drive! Remember, the mind is powerful! We've already established that just by visualizing working out, you can get stronger. Athletes have been using visualization techniques for decades to increase performance. Our thoughts and feelings are the energy that manifests our reality. You can even use social media sites like Pinterest or the wallpaper on your computer as a visual board. My visual board in college had photos of inspiring individuals who made me feel good about myself inside and out. I went on to work in the cosmetic industry, later got a job working at a top motivational company, and then completed all the courses to become a certified trainer.

What you look at day in and day out is powerful. Even if you're in an environment where you can just carry something in your pocket to remind you of beauty, do that. It would help if you constantly were reminded that there is beauty in this world and your future is beautiful. The brain will search its surroundings for opportunities to get you to where you want to be and make the affirmations it absorbs your reality.

Your environment includes the people that you surround yourself with.

One of the most fundamental human needs is the need to

belong. Psychologist Abraham Maslow identified the sense of belonging as one of the five basic human needs. History, psychology, and medical research teach us that humans are wired to be tribal and thrive in loving communities. People who are lonely and unsupported are more likely to be suicidal, suffer depression, or deal with unexplained health and mental issues. Even introverts need a support system to rely on when things get unbearable.

A support group can be as small as one or two people. They can be family, friends, or even an acquaintance who truly understands you. There is nothing better for you than to be surrounded by people who let you be 100% yourself, individuals who love you unconditionally, and who remind you how amazing and beautiful you are, even when you're feeling or acting your ugliest. After all, your support group knows that's when you need them the most. They keep you grounded and confident. If you already have a group or an individual that makes you feel like this, make sure you spend time with them. If you don't, write down the qualities you want such a support group to have. For example, do you need them to treat others with respect, love comedy, science, or mathematics? Would you prefer them to appreciate the arts? Do they need to be loyal? Trustworthy? Have big personalities? Be introverts? After brainstorming the qualities you want, find your people. We tend to connect with people who share the same interest as us.

If you are a charitable person, join a volunteer group in your community. Love rock climbing? Join a meetup group in your area. Love blogging? There are SO many blogging groups on social media on a trillion topics. Rubbing elbows with people of similar interest will expose you to inspiring success stories, expand your library of knowledge, and nurture your creative thinking. Please pay attention to your reaction to others when you meet them. When you meet someone, and you feel you've known that person forever, it's your gut instinct telling you this person should be part of your community. Conversely, when you meet someone and are totally turned off, keep a distance from that person.

As Jim Rohn, one of the most influential motivational speakers, entrepreneurs, and authors, said, "You are the average of the five people you spend the most time with."

Dr. David McClelland, a Harvard social psychologist, says, "The people you habitually associate with determine as much as 95 percent of your success or failure in life."

So, if you want to feel beautiful, make sure you are around confident, thriving, joyful people.

Look around you. *How do you feel about the people and environment you're in?*

"The first step toward success is taken when you refuse to be a captive of the environment in which you first find yourself."
— Mark Caine
(Artificial Intelligence and Machine Learning Lead, World Economic Forum)

───────────

Your dream may be too big for your environment. Don't let the wrong environment crush your dream or stop you from living a life of beauty. Have at least one sacred spot that makes you feel good. Find at least one person to hang out with that inspires you. Keep going until you have a smile on your face for most of your day. Aging *happily ever after* takes work and awareness.

CHAPTER SEVEN

AGING GRACEFULLY

"Look, I wish I could tell you it gets better, but IT doesn't get better. YOU get better."
— Joan Rivers
(Comedian, writer, producer, television host)

HUMANS ARE OBSESSED WITH STOPPING TIME. JUST LOOK AT THE emergence of molecular biology. We are trying to change or control our DNA. While many positive things could come of it, like removing a diabetic, alcoholic, or disease gene, it's motivating some to explore its use to create attractive babies. People are trying to custom order their genetic baby, from selecting the baby's hair and eye color to specifying intelligence level or height.

"There is a time for everything and a season for every activity under the heavens."
Ecclesiastes 3:1

We can't turn every gene of a child off or on as we see fit. Instinctively, at least to me, it's just weird. We may not be able to change the genes that give a person their facial structure now, but what we can change is how we see ourselves at every stage of life. Aging doesn't have to mean you grow old and ugly. That's just a fear. You CAN grow old and beautiful, aging in confidence and authenticity. A verse from the children's book, *The Velveteen Rabbit*, describes it perfectly:

"It doesn't happen all at once, said the Skin Horse. You become. It takes a long time. That's why it doesn't happen often to people who break easily or have sharp edges, or who have to be carefully kept. Generally, by the time you are Real, most of your hair has been loved off, and your eyes drop out, and you get loose in the joints and very shabby. But these things don't matter at all because once you are Real, you can't be ugly, except to people who don't understand."
— Margery Williams Bianco,
The Velveteen Rabbit

What is one guarantee for tomorrow? We all will be a day older. Most of the time, we don't think about this until we get our first wrinkle or grey hair, or we notice our pants are a little snugger.

And then the good fight really starts. We fight to stop the clock or turn it back ten or twenty years. Why? I believe it's fear—fear of being rejected in a world that's obsessed with youth. People want to relive a piece of their carefree twenties that were filled with innocence, hopes, and dreams that may have been extinguished or diminished, or tainted with regret. Knowing that the end is closer than the beginning, the world that was once large and uncertain now feels small and cynical. The only way to avoid these feelings is with a healthy and resilient mind. To keep seeing the beauty about yourself, passion and purpose must never disappear. If you are here, live before you die, express your beauty. The world needs the authentic you. The poem on the next page says it all.

'YOUTH'

Samuel Ullman

"Youth is not a time of life; it is a state of mind; it is not a matter of rosy cheeks, red lips, and supple knees; it is a matter of the will, a quality of the imagination, a vigor of the emotions; it is the freshness of the deep springs of life.

Youth means a temperamental predominance of courage over timidity of the appetite for adventure over the love of ease. This often exists in a man of sixty more than a boy of twenty. Nobody grows old merely by a number of years. We grow old by deserting our ideals.

Years may wrinkle the skin, but to give up enthusiasm wrinkles the soul. Worry, fear, self-distrust bows the heart and turns the spirit back to dust.

Whether sixty or sixteen, there is in every human being's heart the lure of wonder, the unfailing child-like appetite of what's next, and the joy of the game of living. In the center of your heart and my heart, there is a wireless station; so long as it receives messages of beauty, hope, cheer, courage, and power from men and from the infinite, so long are you young.

When the aerials are down, and your spirit is covered with snows of cynicism and the ice of pessimism, then you are grown old, even at twenty, but as long as your aerials are up, to catch the waves of optimism, there is hope you may die young at eighty."

Yes! Yes! Yes! Standing ovation! This piece written by businessman and poet Sam Ullman is what this book is all about. It is a reminder that we should live agelessly as long as we have the mental capacity to live. Never let anyone take beauty out of your life. When people stop growing (or learning), they become old, and life becomes ugly. Age doesn't determine how beautiful we are; a life lived in authenticity does. Telling yourself, you are anything less than beautiful because the outside is aging is so demeaning. Aging should be a celebration of our life experiences and wisdom and the practice of passing our wisdom down to future generations. As time passes, it may diminish our youthful appearance, but it can't take away our youthful glow—unless we let it. We don't have to stop making our life meaningful because we are no longer twenty-five. As the saying goes, *"Don't rest, or you'll rust."* Aging should make us happy inside because it's a gift not afforded to everyone. A wrinkle here and there is an opportunity to put those cosmetics to the test and see if they will really make us look "10 years younger." The longer you get to live, the more chances you are given to discover your beauty, generate more of it, and learn more about this crazy world. One lifetime is not enough to explore all the world has to offer. Take advantage of the years you are given. Every year around the sun is an opportunity to bring something into the world that wasn't here before.

- *James Sinegal founded Costco at 47*
- *Gordon Bowker founded Starbucks at 51*
- *Arianna Huffington started her namesake publication at 55*
- *Vera Wang designed her first dress at 40*
- *Stan Lee created his first comic at 39*
- *Samuel L. Jackson had his most successful role at 43*
- *Momofuku Ando invented instant ramen at 48*

- *Julia Child wrote her first cookbook at 50*
- *Betty White wasn't an icon until 51 when she landed a role in "The Mary Tyler Moore Show."*
- *Ray Kroc spent his career as a milkshake device salesman before buying McDonald's at 52.*
- *Barbara Beskind finally found her dream as a tech designer for IDEO in Silicon Valley at age 91.*
- *According to GEM (Global Entrepreneurship Monitor), The highest rate of entrepreneurship worldwide has shifted to the 55-64 age group.*
- *Five years after startup, 70% of ventures established by 50+ entrepreneurs are still in operation compared to just 28% of enterprises launched by younger entrepreneurs. (GEM)*

It's easy to get lost in the notion that our time is up if we didn't do something in our twenties or thirties. Even from an evolutionary standpoint, the young only count to ensure the reproduction of our species. But evolution doesn't consider how many folks still have emotions and lots of energy at eighty. My grandparents had a ton of energy well into their eighties.

We all want to age gracefully, be happy, and feel as attractive as possible. Though the body may change, our personality stays the same. This makes aging a challenge. And this is definitely why we need to find our inner beauty sooner rather than later. In times past, the elderly and wise were revered. Now the youth are idolized.

To be AGE-LESS, we must accept aging and work on the best version of who we are at 40, 50, 60, and beyond.

The first thing we need to do is step away from the mirror—especially a magnifying mirror. No one, and I mean no one, is going to judge a person that close. When others look at us, we forget that they see expressions, smiles, laughter, and personality—not a dull reflection of pores and wrinkles. My aunt complains all the time about how old and "rugged" she is, but when I look at her, I see so much beauty. It is a sneak peek at what my mother would have looked like. To me, she is super beautiful. We do not know what emotion our appearance may evoke in someone. Research has shown that strangers view us as twenty percent more attractive than we view ourselves. Another study using virtual reality revealed that we find our exact bodies more appealing on an avatar.

This is what Dr. Solene Neyret, the lead author of the study, said: "We also showed that the internal representation that people create of their own body is highly inaccurate. By showing their real body to our female participants from a third-person perspective, we made it appear more attractive to them. We believe that this method can be particularly effective for increasing body satisfaction in patients with eating disorders. One further development of this method would be to use it as a diagnostic tool for body perception disorders."

"We should have the gift of seeing us the way others see us."
— Robert Burns
(Scottish poet and lyricist)

I will not claim that aging is easy because it's not. Like everything in this world, aging gracefully requires action.

Please don't read this as an inspirational book and do nothing. Life loves those who love it back. If you keep living in unproductive anger and envy, you will not have many friends, but you will have a lot of frown lines. Make your goal to become a better version of your beautiful self. There is SO MUCH you can do to age gracefully and stay youthful. It is the inner work that is HARD. You have to work at it EVERY. SINGLE. DAY. Put it into practice; otherwise, this will be another feel-good book.

Remember, children, marriages, and flower gardens reflect the care they get. So does your body, skin, and overall sense of self.

We'd all like to stop time, but until life gives us that gift—or is it even really a gift at all—we have to work with what we have. Strive to be a beautiful person, not just beautiful to look at. You'll end up unforgettable and happy. Most people living off their image get replaced by the next pretty face when they can no longer sell the face cream. But the *'unforgettables,'* as I call them, dwell with you your entire life.

The *unforgettables* know the ultimate form of beauty is *happiness*. They use cosmetics to enhance their appearance and happiness to pamper their soul. *Unforgettable*s know that true happiness can only be enjoyed by those who balance their inside and out. Happiness is found when you follow what makes your soul (true self) happy. If you do not understand who you are, you will continue searching for the next cosmetic, or relationship, or ad that defines it for you. Those without a strong sense of self will keep depending on an image in the media, usually a lot younger than they are. We all know where that leads-just Google bad plastic surgery.

Aging joyfully is timeless. Happiness is the best Botox. A genuine smile lifts everything up.

Photographer Marcus Alberti put together a project where he invited several friends of different ages over one week. He took pictures of them after the first, second, and third glass of wine. In the first photos, you see them guarding themselves, trying to look good for the photo, tense, a little insecure, small smiles, and reflecting all the stress from their daily life in their faces and body language. By the third glass of wine, they all have big smiles and a light about them that makes you feel like you'd want to hang out with those people. He captured genuine silliness and happiness. They all looked a few years younger. The last photo on all subjects increased in attractiveness by fifty percent, regardless of their ages. I am not saying to down a bottle of wine to find happiness because after three glasses, oh my gosh, we go from pretty to pretty drunk. What I am saying is, find something that makes you relax (like wine).

Find the hobbies and people that make you subconsciously set your phone down and smile and laugh. When you are engaged in a pursuit you love, genuine facial expressions happen. Your inner soul shines through. Your guard of self-judgment is let down. Be social and make friends. Not only is it good for your brain, but people also find you more attractive once they get to know you. Think about all your friends. You don't care how they look. Meaningful friendships transcend the boundaries of image and create a feeling of infinite beauty—heart, mind, body. As we grow older, relationships become even more critical.

People who have more social support have better mental health, cardiovascular health, immunological function, and cognitive performance. The well-known, long-running Harvard Medical School Nurses' Health Study was one of the early studies to reveal how being socially integrated can lead to greater health, life satisfaction, and longevity. Researchers who conducted another study involving nearly 7,000 people over nine years found that those with more social ties live longer regardless of their socioeconomic status, smoking, drinking, exercise, or obesity. So, find friends and keep playing. Be silly. Make people feel good about themselves. Every woman should feel the same sense of beauty they had at five years old.

BECOME A KID AGAIN. A kid wants to love and know they are loved, and I believe that is what adults want. It's one of the reasons we crave being attractive. We believe being attractive is to be adored. But the real trick is to love, love, love. Be kind. Play, smile, find something hidden about yourself that you didn't know was even there.

> *"We don't stop playing because we grow old; we grow old because we stop playing."*
> *— George Bernard Shaw*

You must feel beautiful to be beautiful. Pay close attention to what you admire. What you admire about someone else, you already have in yourself, which is why you're able to notice it. Discover it! What you see is what you want to be, or the opposite, you need to fix. Let people know your story of overcoming. It took you a long time to get where you are, and you're still standing strong. Loving yourself doesn't mean ignoring the heartbreak and flaws. It means learning from them and still loving yourself despite it all because you know deep down that you are more than a 'look' with more than a past. If you genuinely love yourself, the flame can't be put out by someone else's lack of admiration—and there is nothing more attractive than that.

"It is the old apple trees that are decked with the loveliest blossoms. It is the ancient redwoods that rise to majestic heights. It is the old violins that produce the richest tones. It is the aged wine that tastes the sweetest. It is ancient coins, stamps, and furniture that people seek. It is the old friends that are loved the best. Thank God for the blessings of age and the wisdom, patience, and maturity that goes with it."
Steve Goodier
(Author of *Lessons of the Turtle: Living Right Side Up*)

Age isn't an excuse to deny who you are. Keep learning, keep following the voice that says, "There is more." Strengthen the relationship between your mind and body. Train your inner beauty to take over by focusing on it. Once you are on the right path, your bliss will open more doors for you.

"When we die and go to meet our maker, we are not going to be asked why we didn't become a messiah or find a cure for cancer. Instead, we will be asked, "Why didn't you become you?"
Elie Wiesel
(Author of Souls on Fire)

CHAPTER EIGHT

THE TRUTH ABOUT COSMETICS

NOW THAT WE'VE EXPLORED REAL BEAUTY, LET'S TALK ALL about image and the fundamental truths of cosmetics. Appearance is important, BUT only after we get the beauty part right. I repeat, **BEAUTY MUST COME FIRST.** Balance your life in a way that your inner beauty always outshines your external appearance. If the exterior is prettier, focus on the interior STAT! We will never be beautiful until we are truly authentic. An image we feel comfortable in only allows us to express our inner beauty more easily.

We gain more confidence to go out into the world. Even dressing up and putting on makeup have benefits. The "lipstick effect" is a known psychological phenomenon in which wearing makeup can give individuals a confidence boost by making them feel more physically attractive, increasing self-esteem, positivity, and overall self-assurance. And a boost in self-esteem can also boost cognitive abilities. This is why I do not diminish the importance of looking good. Just understand that the beauty within is far greater than what people see on the outside. Image is the easy part IF you're right within. You've already read about the benefits of healing the mind. Being attractive on the outside is easier than you think.

Guess what? You don't need fifty-million products and procedures to look good. There are basics you need to understand.

1. HOW TO KEEP SKIN CLEAR
2. BASIC ANTI-AGING INGREDIENTS THAT WORK
3. DIET
4. STRESS REDUCTION

Anti-aging, what a concept! It always cracks me up when I see "erase ten years in fourteen days." Okay, but what if I put it on a newborn? Claims are catchy but generally not true. The effects of aging are inevitable; however, we can make it a positive experience if we instill in our minds that aging is natural, how we evolve, and not everyone is privileged to do it.

We are a society that will try anything to stop the wrinkles of time. Some dermatologists even suggest that the overuse of cosmetics is increasing the occurrence of sensitive skin in people. Mixing different ingredients and using too much of a product, especially with a lot of additives, can break down the protective barrier of the skin. Women use cosmetics more than men, and men are less likely to have sensitive skin. Women need to be very careful with the products they choose. The goal is to beautify, not break down. To enhance the outside, first, find out what skin type you have and focus on products only for issues you're having.

Normal skin. Normal skin is balanced with the proper amount of oil. It is not too dry or too oily. Normal skin lacks redness and rarely has breakouts.

Dry skin. Dry skin is flaky, itchy, or rough.

Oily skin. Oily skin is shiny, greasy, and prone to acne and breakouts.

Combination skin. Combination skin has areas that are dry and oily. For example, the forehead, nose, or chin might be oily, but the cheeks are dry.

Sensitive skin. Sensitive skin is susceptible to irritation, redness, itching, or rashes.

Mature skin. Mature skin shows signs of loss of elasticity, fine lines, wrinkles, and dark spots.

And just because something claims to be all-natural doesn't mean you can bombard your skin with it. The term natural is increasing in unnatural significance. Arsenic is natural. Cyanide is natural. Queen Elizabeth used lead as a skin whitener and lost her teeth and hair. The three major elements to maintaining "flawless" skin are: understanding and managing breakouts, keeping pores a normal size, and slowing the wrinkling process.

How Breakouts Happen:

Pores don't go on attack breaking your skin out because they don't like you. Breakouts happen because of accumulated impurities, like dirt and oil. Without pores, you would be bald, your complexion would be dull and dehydrated, and you would die of heat exhaustion. If you really want your pores to disappear, you're going to disappear too. If all your pores closed up, you would literally dry up.

Pores are small openings in the skin that release oils and sweat. They're also connected to your hair follicles. Wherever there is hair, there are pores. That's why breakouts can happen all over the body. The tiny openings (pores) allow sweat, sebum, and dead skin cells to exit the skin's surface. The dead skin cells and sebum coat and protect skin from bacteria and viruses and condition the skin.

Sweat is there to regulate body temperature. As skin gets hotter, pores dilate, and sweat exits to the surface. The evaporation of the sweat cools the skin. In a perfect world, dead skin cells, sweat, and sebum would exit smoothly onto the skin, but that is not always the case. Sometimes, pores get clogged with debris such as makeup, dirt, or dried-up dead skin cells that have hardened on the skin's surface. The material that clogs the pores stops sebum, sweat, and dead skin cells from exiting the surface; then, bacteria accumulates underneath the skin's surface. The accumulation alerts the immune system that foreign objects in the body are causing infections. The immune system releases white blood cells to obstruct, which causes the skin to inflame. This inflammation is characterized by heat, swelling, redness, and pain and is seen on the skin's surface as acne, whiteheads, and blackheads.

If the pores stay clogged, acne can get worse, especially if a person has oily skin. The overproduction of oil attracts more dirt and bacteria under the skin, and the buildup can cause deeper infections, and an abscess will develop. If acne does occur, it's imperative that blackheads, whiteheads, and acne are left alone and not squeezed. Squeezing may lead to a little scarring, which widens pores. No matter what the cosmetic companies tell you, genetics determine the size of your pores. Pores don't permanently get bigger and smaller or open and close because of a moisturizer, although certain conditions can make it seem that way.

Oily skin has wider oil ducts, creating the illusion of bigger pores on the surface. Products that contain acetone and alcohol will shrink pores temporarily. Acetone and alcohol irritate the skin surface, which causes swelling around the pore, thus creating a smaller pore. However, this is short-lived, and the pore will go back to its natural size. Sunburns do the same thing. Sunburned skin becomes inflamed and swells. But once the inflammation subsides, the pores go back to their natural size. That being said, keep skin acne-free, fresh, and vibrant. When pores are clear, they appear smaller and smoother. It is important that pores are kept their normal size and unclogged. Here are a few tips:

1. It's mandatory that makeup and other products are oil-free, non-comedogenic, and dermatologist-tested. Look for products that say non-comedogenic, as these are products with ingredients that have shown they do not clog pores.

2. Wash all products off before going to bed. If the skin is oily, wash your face at least twice a day.

3. Always wear sunblock. The sun thickens cells around the pores, creating the illusion of bigger pores.

4. Use medications that contain salicylic acid to dry up the overproduction of oil.

5. For other skin types, products with vitamin A are an excellent way of keeping the skin free of dead skin cells.

6. And lastly, use a daily exfoliant. It will remove the dirt, oil, and other debris that has accumulated throughout the day that clog and distend the pores. With regular care and maintenance, your skin can be "PORE-FECT."

"Inside every older person is a younger person wondering what the hell happened?!?"
— *Unknown*

How the Skin Ages:

There is nothing worse than feeling like a vibrant, youthful *cougar* ready to pounce from the inside until you look in the mirror and see a broken down, pre-historic mountain lion. Really, who wants that?! And though the cosmetic companies love that you spend billions of dollars a year on anti-aging creams, the best way to protect from an empty wallet and wrinkled skin is to prevent wrinkles and damage in the first place.

Unless you're a vampire or dating one who can bite you into youthfulness, avoid the sun, especially between the hours of 10 AM and 2 PM when the sun's rays are the strongest. It's essential to use an SPF 30 or higher, and don't forget the ears and lips. I stop at SPF 30 because studies have shown there's no proof of better protection over that rating. Also, remember that after sugar, the next cause of uneven skin tone, age spots, and premature wrinkles is the sun.

According to Web MD, "Over time, the sun's ultraviolet light damages the fibers in the skin called elastin. When these fibers break down, the skin sags stretches, and loses its ability to go back into place after stretching." Basically, the sun turns you into a Shar-Pei if you're not careful.

Every 28-45 days, skin cells renew themselves, revealing fresher, brighter, younger-looking skin. However, as we age, this process slows down, and old cells pile up on the skin's surface, creating a dull, rough, and dry complexion. Even worse, dead skin cells clog pores leading to blemishes and acne. Not to mention, your $100 moisturizer will no longer penetrate through the skin. Weekly exfoliation is vital to help rid the skin of cells that are not renewing fast enough.

There are many exfoliation methods, such as cleansers, retinol creams, machines, chemical peels, microdermabrasion, and more. You'll want to choose a method according to your skin type. Most women over-cleanse and treat their skin. We only need a few products:

1. A good moisturizing cleanser—yes, even if your skin is oily.
2. A chemical-free SPF of at least 30.
3. A night moisturizer targeting your biggest aging concerns.
4. A serum and retinol.

In addition, I recommend a separate eye crème if you have wrinkles or dark and puffy eyes.

The Proper Way To Apply Products—In This Order:

1.*Serum:* Serums will stick to dirt and dead skin. For maximum absorption, cleanse the face thoroughly, and while skin is still damp, massage two pea-size drops of your favorite serum over your face for 60 seconds.

2.*Retinol cream:* To reduce irritation, wait 20 minutes after washing the face before applying retinoids to the skin. Using a retinoid cream on damp skin will cause it to absorb faster, increasing the chances of redness and irritated skin. Retinol, especially prescription retinol, will lose its effectiveness in sunlight. It should only be applied at night. Less is more. Apply two pea size dabs over your face and one pea-size amount on the neck and chest.

3.*Moisturizer:* If you have noticeably dry skin, use a moisturizer twice a day. If you have oily skin, use it once a day, preferably at night. Pay close attention to the cheeks and area around the mouth, as they tend to be the driest. It's best to apply moisturizer on damp skin to trap moisture on the surface. Pat and massage for 60 seconds. DON'T RUB!

4.*Sunscreen:* To ensure complete protection when applying sunscreen, start with about a quarter size amount and apply on the outside of the face first near the hair and jawline and move inward.

5.*Eye Cream:* Apply a pea-size amount of eye cream under the eyes and on the UPPER lid close to the brow bone. Cream travels at least an inch downward after applied, so if you apply directly to the lower lid or near the lash line, the cream will get into the eyes and could make them irritated or puffy. Always apply eye creams with your ring finger, as it's your weakest finger.

Prevention Saves Money

To age gracefully, your mind must work right; you must treat it right. Diet and exercise are probably the most essential part of your day. You knew it was coming. After all, the body is the shelter for all the beauty inside. You've got to take care of it.

I don't know everything there is about dieting, and this isn't everyone's truth. Some people may have medical issues that require a specific diet. But for most healthy people, I don't recommend a diet at all. I hate the word "diet." There are TOOOOO many of them. To me, a diet is marketed as something you can try for a little while until you lose weight, and then you are free to carry on with your past lifestyle. That's why so many people regain weight after a trending diet.

A balanced lifestyle change is the only way to stay consistent. Find the minerals and vitamins your own body is lacking and replenish them. You can ask your doctor for a vitamin deficiency test. If you're overweight, unfortunately, it is decreasing food intake that will help you the most. Calorie restriction is better at helping to maintain weight than exercise. We try everything to avoid this one truth because we love food. But it is the truth. Most of us are overeating. We celebrate with food. We stress eat, binge eat, have snacks with our favorite show, and even sneak food off other people's plates. Overeating is the number one cause of weight gain. And unhealthy calories lead to not only weight gain but wrinkles and disease. It ages us in warp speed.

This is the hardest pill to swallow, especially for hormonal women craving sweets, but we must be consciously aware of making smarter choices. Everything we eat not only has an effect on our waistline but our skin. And the biggest skin destroyer is sugar! If I could give you one piece of diet advice, it's avoiding added sugar, and if possible, sugar altogether.

Sugar is the number one aging agent. It damages the skin through a process known as glycation. When you eat sugar, it goes into the bloodstream, attaches to proteins, and produces harmful free radicals called advanced glycation end (AGEs) products, which accumulate every time you eat sugar and damage the "protector" proteins around them. AGEs are dangerous. They prevent your kidney from filtering toxins properly, cause cardiovascular diseases, and wreak all sorts of damage that makes your body age and fall sick faster. Your skin isn't immune to it. Here's how glycation makes your skin age faster:

1. **Destroys collagen:** AGEs alter the structure of collagen, making it stiff and inflexible.
2. **Inflames skin:** AGEs trigger inflammation, the #1 cause of wrinkles and premature aging.
3. **Gives you dark spots:** AGEs can affect skin discoloration.

Glycation in diabetics has been reversed after balancing sugar levels. The legendary dermatologist Dr. Fredric Brandt used to say that giving up sugar could make you look younger by ten years.

In a lab test, the more sugar fed to animals, the older their skin gets. Stress makes us hungry. It signals the hormone cortisol, which tells the brain we're hungry, and we reach for fatty, sugary foods. Awareness of this trigger will help.

What are your go-to foods? I love dark chocolate, but I eat eighty percent cacao with no added sugar. I try to keep my sugar intake to a maximum of 25 grams per day. I notice that when I'm traveling or in a mood where I want to splurge, I gain weight quickly. Sugar is in everything, and there are different types of sugars. The one you want to avoid most is sucrose (added white sugar).

The four most common forms of simple sugars include:

- Glucose (blood sugar)
- Fructose (fruit sugar)
- Sucrose (table sugar)
- Lactose (dairy sugar)

Excess is the biggest health problem we are facing today. Added sugar in moderation is fine, but most people consume much more than they realize. In the Standard American Diet (SAD), top sources of added sugar include soda, fruit drinks, cereals, cookies, cakes, candy, flavored yogurts, and many processed foods. According to the American Heart Association, American adults consume an average of 77 grams of added sugar per day. Ultimately, the fewer calories and sugar you ingest, the better your skin and health.

Reduce Stress.

Lastly, no one can feel or look beautiful if they are stressed out. When have you heard anyone say, *"Wow, look at that girl ripping her hair out and banging her head up against the wall, SO BEAUTIFUL?!"* Stress sucks. And we don't take care of ourselves the way we should when we're stressed. I, for one, reach for the carbs when I'm stressed. Pizza, please. I do not tend to take care of my skin as well, either. In my times of stress, I have found that even five minutes of deep breathing significantly helps relax my body and tame the crazy cravings I'm going to regret. Deep breathing has been proven to lower blood pressure, increase serotonin (the happy hormone), and improve the immune system. YES—in just 5 minutes! Like the gurus of Namaste say, "The more you meditate, the more you radiate."

Research from the University of Sheffield that combines already proven studies found that techniques like meditation, relaxation sessions, and cognitive behavior therapy benefits people suffering from skin conditions like psoriasis, eczema, acne, and vitiligo (a pigment disorder). In one study, people who suffered from psoriasis listened to meditation tapes while receiving ultraviolet light treatments. The result? They healed *four times faster* than non-meditators. The study determined that meditation reduced the stress that caused psoriasis in the first place and triggered the body's innate ability to repair itself. Reduced stress equals better skin.

We can scientifically reduce stress with nature's super drug: the mind. The more you meditate, the more often you reach a higher consciousness, thereby projecting a feeling of tranquility to those around you. Anyone who feels this with you will know you've found your inner beauty.

I didn't believe the hype on meditation myself until I started doing it. I began to realize my fear of evolving into old age. But during mediation, I began to see how powerful the body really is, how capable it is to heal itself. I saw a shift in my whole thought process. If you sit quietly long enough, answers come to you. I am an anxious person, so quieting the mind is a little tricky, but I learned to acknowledge those thoughts. You realize that even the negative ones have a purpose. Meditate for 30 days, even if it's only five minutes a day, and watch the subtle transformation in your face. It's pretty cool to see.

Brow lines and forehead wrinkles (from frowning) are less pronounced. The soul is ageless; meditation helps you remember that. It enables you to find your inner being that the outside has imperceptibly taken over. I recommend sitting in front of a mirror for a few minutes just staring at yourself. Keep a meditation journal with you and document the positive and negative thoughts that come to you during your sessions. This will help you identify what you need to heal from and meditate on in future meditations. Meditate until you can look at a mirror for five minutes with complete self-acceptance. I have noticed mature meditators who make the practice a part of their lifestyle **look decades younger** than their "true" age, and they have a longer life span. My goal is to become an experienced meditator.

The Exploration of Consciousness Research Institute (EOC Institute) has several articles on the miracle benefits of meditation. Backed by 117,000 peer-reviewed scientific studies, meditation has been shown to boost *glutathione* (GSH), anointed as the "mother of all antioxidants." Gustavo Bounous, MD, retired McGill University professor, told Medicinenet.com that: "It's the [body's] most important antioxidant because it's within the cell [which is a prime position to neutralize free radicals]." Jeremy Appleton, ND, a naturopathic physician and respected author, was recently quoted: "If you look in a hospital situation at people who have cancer, AIDS, or other very serious diseases, almost invariably they are depleted in glutathione. The reasons for this are not completely understood, but we do know that glutathione is extremely important for maintaining intracellular health."

Glutathione not only stops oxidative stress but also plays a helper role for many critical enzymes, fights cancer by slowing apoptosis (programmed cell death), boosts t-cells, shields environmental toxin damage, and guards against drug resistance, all while supercharging immunity.

The thing is, GSH is not well-absorbed into the body when taken as a supplement (capsule). While intravenous results are more promising, there is no need to become a pincushion. Why? Because meditation supercharges your body with glutathione! The EOC mentions a well-cited 51-person study published in the Journal of Alternative and Complementary Medicine (Sinha et al. 2007) that showed that, alongside yoga, meditation boosts this powerhouse peptide by a whopping 41%! Another antioxidant increase that results from meditation is nitric oxide. Your brain, arteries, immune system, liver, pancreas, and lungs would quickly shut down without this incredible stuff.

Further, the more you have to flow through your beautiful body, the longer you will live. Health care research has proven that people don't change out of fear but from reward. Meditation offers a lot of rewards. Consider too that taking a meditative walk outside in nature decreases cortisol and belly fat without dieting. (Yale University)

Age is nothing but an invisible number. God gave us all a unique fingerprint so we can leave an imprint that no one else can. Our purpose doesn't stop at 25, and it doesn't flinch at wrinkles or pump the brakes if our skin isn't flawless.

CHAPTER NINE

TOP TEN BEAUTY SECRETS FOR SKIN, MAKEUP, BODY, AND MIND

"The most beautiful makeup of a woman is passion. But cosmetics are easier to buy."

— *Yves Saint Laurent*
(Fashion designer)

I HAVE WORKED ALL OVER, FROM THE TINIEST OF TOWNS IN Idaho to the Hollywood Hills in California and, as writer Jean-Baptiste Alphonse Karr wrote, *"plus ça change, plus c'est la même chose" "The more things change, the more they remain the same."* This is especially true when it comes to our exterior image. No matter how crazy the cosmetic world becomes, from scary tips online like using a permanent marker as eyeliner (DO NOT DO THIS) to the rise of girls as young as 16 wanting butt implants- eventually, when authenticity kicks in, we tend to resort back to the beautiful world of simplicity. Here is my top ten list that I promised you for makeup, body, and mind that I learned over ten years working in the cosmetic world. It all goes back to the basics. They still ring true and prominent dermatologists recommend some of them themselves!

Skin

1. Get at least seven hours of sleep, eight if you can. Anything less than seven doesn't give the body time to repair itself, and side effects like dark eyes and sallow-looking skin will show themselves.

> *"You cannot treat the skin as an isolated organ; you treat the whole person. Imagine your window frame needs to be replaced. You can just replace the frame, or you can find out what damaged it in the first place, say termites or bad plumbing. Similarly, when the skin looks gray and sallow, and you have dark circles around your eyes, you can use cold compresses and makeup as a temporary fix, or address the underlying issues, such as sleep deprivation."*
> — *Dr. Murad*, M.D., F.A.A.D

2. Wear an SPF of at least 30+. The American Dermatology Association (ADA) recommends one that's labeled "broad-spectrum" because this means it protects against both UVA and UVB rays. UVA rays are the ones that prematurely age your skin, causing wrinkles and age spots, while UVB rays cause sunburn. Overexposure to either can lead to skin cancer.

. . .

3. For the best anti-aging moisturizer, look for ones with a vitamin A derivative such as retinol and retinaldehydes. The next most effective ingredient to look for is L-ascorbic acid.

4. Cheeks are the driest part of the face. Make sure to apply more moisturizer to that area first.

5. Add turmeric to any face mask. It will brighten the skin and lighten dark spots. Turmeric regulates the production of melanin.

6. I have seen wonderful outcomes from *Sea Salt* Microdermabrasion. During my time in the cosmetic world, the women who had glowing skin always got these facials.

7. Use safflower oil for wrinkles. It is high in linoleic acid. In as little as two weeks, it will start to plump up the skin. I know it works. This is one of my go-to's!

8. Every few months, get glycolic peels (unless you have super sensitive skin).

9. Use an oil-based face wash; all skin types. There are no harsh ingredients in oil cleaners. Oils are super soothing, excellent at removing makeup, and they tame unrelenting breakouts.

10. Dry brush the whole body and face once a week. It takes off old skin cells, increases blood flow, increasing circulation, which can help with cellulite and smooth the skin.

Hair

1. Use coconut oil on the hair. Once a week, rub it in your hair in the evening and shampoo in the morning. It's proven to strengthen hair and prevent split ends, making hair stronger and thicker. It also kills fungus and loosens dry skin on the scalp.

2. Wash hair only every other day—or less—to increase its natural oils. Use Natural Dry Shampoo for days you don't wash. Spray the dry shampoo at the roots and blow-dry through to

remove more grease and dirt. This practice slows color fade and minimizes damage.

3. For volume, add a teaspoon of salt to the shampoo. That's what's in those special salt shampoos.

4. Shower caps! After shampooing, put on your conditioner and place a shower cap over your head. The heat from the shower will help penetrate the hair shaft to soften textured hair.

5. Add flour to your conditioner if you want to increase the volume of the hair. Oat flour is a great one. Add a few tablespoons of oat flour to your conditioner after shampooing. Your hair will be shiny and smooth in an instant — with the benefit of added volume — as the flour helps make the brittle strands of your hair look thicker.

6. Condition, Condition, Condition! Start at the ends. This is where hair is the weakest. Let the conditioner sit for a minute or two. Add vinegar to your conditioner for shine. Most conditioners work well; avoid any products with alcohol in them.

7. Invest in a quality brush. A quality brush really does make a difference. Boar brushes are best for dry hair.

8. Eat foods high in essential fatty acids. Deficiency in essential fatty acids can result in hair loss.

9. Blow dry on low heat and ALWAYS use a leave-in conditioner on hair ends before blow-drying.

10. Trim dead ends every six weeks to keep them from splitting.

Diet

1. If you crave something sweet, take a bite of a pickle. It shuts down the urge to splurge on the sweet stuff.

2. Drink a little coffee. A single cup of coffee contains 11% of the daily recommended value of riboflavin (vitamin B2). A riboflavin deficiency can cause the skin to become excessively

oily. Coffee also contains pantothenic acid (vitamin B5), manganese, niacin, and magnesium—all anti-aging antioxidants.

3. Eat foods with niacin. Several studies show that products containing niacin can stimulate DNA repair, boost hydration, increase ceramide production, and increase cell turnover. (Some foods high in niacin are grass-fed beef, salmon, sardines, avocado, organic brown rice).

4. Eat spinach. It's loaded with vitamin K. This vitamin can increase a protein that strengthens blood vessels, stopping icky spider veins in their tracks.

5. Sprinkle cinnamon on coffee and foods. It shrinks fat cells, and it's a proven metabolism booster shrinking fat in the abdomen.

6. Take sugar out of your mouth and put it on your face. Sugar's disinfectant properties banish pimples that cause bacteria and heal blemishes. Mix sugar with water to form a paste, massage for 10-15 seconds, and rinse.

7. Eat fruit. A Stanford University study showed that women who eat two cups of fruit daily feel more optimistic and energized in as little as seventy-two hours.

8. Eat walnuts. They're loaded with arginine, which relaxes blood vessels, and omega three, which fights the inflammation that causes under-eye bags.

9. Sniff grapefruit before you eat. The scent can curb your appetite in less than sixty-seconds, making you eat fewer calories. And if you wear a grapefruit scent, you'll be perceived as younger.

10. Eat avocado. They're good for the skin and can boost mood as well as antidepressants.

. . .

Bonus: Eat foods loaded with water. We get the benefits of the minerals, vitamins, and fiber in the food. Not to mention, our bodies absorb water more slowly from food, and it stays in our bodies longer. Just one cup of watermelon raises your body's store of the amino acid arginine. Great news because arginine burns fat and builds lean muscle!

ATTN: Monday desk junkies!!! Researchers discovered that when people sit all day, their buttock cells enlarge and form fat droplets. After just two weeks of prolonged sitting, scientists noticed that the stretched cells produced more and bigger fat droplets increasing a person's butt size, even if they tend to play sports or work out! Make sure you're getting up at least every half hour!

Makeup

Fun Fact: in 1770, the British parliament banned red lipstick, saying it had the power to seduce men into marriage and classified it as witchcraft.

---

1. Wear eyeliner that makes your eye color pop. For example, a bronze liner will make green eyes stand out—purple for brown and hazel.
2. Wear a little blush. It brightens the whole face.
3. Avoid using products with phenol. It strips the top layer of your lip (natural protection).
4. Put a clear mascara on before regular mascara. It

separates the regular mascara, making it darker and shiner.

5. Apply a little champagne color in the inner corner of the eye. It will brighten the eyes and make them bigger and brighter.

6. To create a nice dimension on the eyes and make them stand out, use two similar colors, but different, like dark and light purple on the lids.

7. Curl the lashes. It's the easiest way to open the eyes.

8. Most foundations wear off fast because women tend to choose the wrong foundations for their skin type. Dry skin types should use a moisturizing foundation and add an oil-based sunblock or any soothing oil before application. The oil will act as a barrier between the skin and makeup, keeping the foundation from seeping into lines. Oily skin types should use clay-based foundations. They're the best at controlling makeup robbing oil. To help foundation last even longer, add a face primer targeted for your skin type before applying foundation.

9. Your face is three-dimensional, so applying foundation in a single tone will only make your face appear flat. Add a highlighter to areas of your face that would usually catch light but create enough shadow to emphasize your jawline and cheekbones.

10. Exfoliation is an important and easy way to buff away dead skin cells that cover up your skin's natural glow. Use a light exfoliator to take off any residue and dry skin before applying makeup.

Mind

1. Meditate.
2. Read. According to a study at Rus University Medical Center, regularly reading reduces memory problems by 32%.
3. Find a purpose bigger than yourself. (EGO)
4. Study ancient text and women who are stronger with their minds than their image.
5. Get an essential oil diffuser. U.K. researchers have found just smelling bergamot orange essential oil triggers GABA production. GABA lowers stress.
6. Watch something inspiring or comical first thing in the morning. It will set the tone for your day.
7. Be mindful of your thoughts. Listen to anxious thoughts. Don't try to push them away. Acknowledging that they are there helps you get rid of them faster. Ask yourself how rational they are. Is there anything you can do? They will pass.
8. Listen to music. Case in point, according to Dr. David Lewis-Hodgson of Mindlab International, the song "Weightless" by Marconi Union can reduce anxiety levels by up to 65%.
9. Ride out emotions. Don't block them. Acknowledge them and cry if you need to. Suppressed emotions create negative energy on the whole.
10. Take a walk. Research in a growing scientific field called Ecotherapy has shown a strong connection between time spent in nature and reduced stress, anxiety, and depression.

CHAPTER TEN

IN CONCLUSION

THE JOURNEY TO BEAUTY: UPS, DOWNS, INSECURITIES, confidence, judgment, hate, love, indifference, compassion, and acceptance—(Transformation to higher self).

Here is a summary of where I want you to focus.

Be aware of how you speak to yourself.

Negative self-talk increases anxiety and depression. There is too much research out there about the body and mind connection. It would be foolish to ignore it. The body responds in ugly ways when you spend your days telling yourself you're ugly or not good enough. Try to focus away from comparing yourself to others and acknowledging what makes you, YOU—the spark in the world no one else can ignite. **DON'T WASTE YOUR GIFTS.**

The spirit of beauty is everywhere.

No one lacks it. They only lack the ability to see it.

As in all important matters, awareness is key. We need to take the time to acknowledge any internal reasons we lack to see the beauty on the outside. Once you start to notice beauty, keep a journal to document the beauty you encounter or experience. Read it at the end of the week. Whenever I feel like the world is getting dark, I pull out my journal. What I have written reminds me of all the beauty that can be experienced at any moment. I have journaled about strangers who spoke words so inspiring they answered prayers for me without even realizing it, to descriptions of the Palace of Versailles in the Île-de-France region of France. Both experiences different, but both beautiful. I have written about the beauty that is given to us daily, a sunset and sunrise. In these moments, I see God's art.

I will never forget the feeling I got watching the sunset as I stood over the Grand Canyon. The colors changed vividly from orange to pink, to purple, while I stood in silence, mind clear, wholly engaged at the moment, surrounded by nature's light show; ethereal is the only way to describe it. Or the sunrise I experienced in Assisi, Italy, the birthplace of St. Francis. I remember hearing the spiritual sounds of bell chimes. I opened the window and watched the sun slowly illuminate this otherworldly valley. It was one of the most substantial feelings of ethereal beauty I've ever experienced, other than the birth of my child. I felt the *presence* of peace for the first time in my life. These are all written down and inspire me every time I read them. Life is meant to be noticed, studied, and appreciated. We are only meant to add to the beauty for others to see. Beauty can be something as simple as a word spoken. Some words I find beautiful are:

Meraki— Greek word for doing things with love, passion, and a lot of soul.
Gökotta— Swedish word meaning to rise at dawn in order to listen to early morning birdsong.
Komorebi—Japanese word for describing the interplay between light and leaves when sunlight shines through trees.

READ READ READ

Read about people you admire, inspiring quotes, literature, self-improvement books, fiction, ancient text, The Bible, poetry… just keep reading. You will become more educated, interesting, and learn stuff you never even knew you were interested in—and a big bonus, you're more likely to become rich. Self-made millionaire Steve Siebold interviewed 1,200 of the world's wealthiest people to find out what traits they shared. One trait all of them had in common is their passion for reading everything from self-improvement books to autobiographies. Research published in the Journal of American Academy of Neurology finds that people who engage in mentally stimulating activities like reading experience slower memory decline than those who do not.

A reader lives a thousand lives before he dies…. The man who never reads lives only one. — George R. R. Martin (Author of the series of epic fantasy novels A Song of Ice and Fire, which was adapted into the Emmy Award-winning HBO series Game of Thrones)

Read or watch something that makes you laugh or inspires you first thing in the morning.

"Orient yourself properly. Then—and only then—concentrate on the day. Set your sights at the Good, the Beautiful, and the True, and then focus pointedly and carefully on the concerns of each moment. Aim continually at Heaven while you work diligently on Earth. Attend fully to the future, in that manner, while attending fully to the present. Then you have the best chance of perfecting both."

— Jordan Peterson

(Professor of psychology at the University of Toronto, a clinical psychologist, and YouTube personality).

"A Smile is the best facelift."

One can never feel unattractive while laughing. FACT. And a good belly laugh does wonders for the abs. Laughing first thing in the morning will set a positive tone and raise your positive vibes. You'll notice more positive things happening around you when you are happy. I love *dad jokes,* and I love to tell them. The priceless look on people's faces of "Will this ever stop?" is cheerful in itself. Some of my favorite ones are:

A bear walks into a bar and says, "Give me a whiskey… and a cola." "Why the big 'pause'?" asks the bartender.

The bear shrugged. "I'm not sure. I was born with them."

Did you hear about the claustrophobic astronaut?

He just needed a little space.

Why are pirates called pirates?

Because they *arrgh!*

. . .

HAHAHA! Okay. Okay. You get the point. I'll stop. I also watch my favorite stand-up comedians or listen to a playlist of upbeat music. The vibe you set in the morning is the most important.

Strive to Be Unforgettable.

Remember, the "It" girl will get replaced by the next attractive face or trending feature. It is the "unforgettables" who dwell with us our entire lives. The *unforgettables* remind us that beauty is HAPPINESS, and happiness is a balance of the inner and outer self. What a tragedy if you spend the days of your life chasing a look and forgetting your gifts. Beauty and authenticity transcend the materials of this world.

Know thyself.

Constructive criticism is good.

With thyself, beauty is not in the beholder's eye, but the mind. Heal the past and take awareness to where you may still be self-sabotaging. There is a difference between constructive criticism and being critical. Surround yourself with those who use constructive words. Remember, you can't fix what you can't see. Constructive criticism is helpful and a blessing. You will know it is CONSTRUCTIVE when a pattern of the same weakness is pointed out by those closest to you. It is a wonderful way to see where the soul may need a little polishing. The head does not rule the heart, but you need to calm the head to get to the heart.

"If you are irritated by every rub, then how will you be polished"- Rumi

---

Stop the desperate search for perfection.
RIGHT NOW.

We live in a material world, but you don't have to be a material girl. Brands need to sell products to make money, and the only way to do that is to create the illusion that you NEED their product. The increasing pressure of maintaining one's appearance is inescapable, as methods and products are constantly advertised to aid women in their quest for perfection, which doesn't exist. I have nothing against maintaining and preventing aging. You would be silly not too. If a woman is right on the inside and wants a little nip and tuck to keep things looking good, believe me, I'm all for that. But ultimately, trying to change who you are is where things turn scary on the outside. The normal woman doesn't have millions of dollars lying around to go to the top surgeons. Out of desperation, she will get coupons for discounted and botched surgery if she isn't careful.

The trouble with striving to be a social image is, it's constantly changing. It used to be about the biggest boobs. Currently, it's about the butt. Not all trends look good on people's natural body type, and looks don't translate universally. You'll forever be on a journey of non-existing perfection. The best thing to do is pick two of your best features and enhance them naturally. Eventually, chasing perfection will empty your wallet, make you look like a plastic version of someone else, or cause you stress, making you look and feel worse, all while destroying you physically and depleting you psychologically. Let's face it: perfection rarely occurs in this world, and as Russian novelist, Leo Tolstoy pointed out, "If you look for perfection, you will never be content." Too many women work on perfection and not self-acceptance. Perfection is an illusion; self-acceptance creates happiness. Yes, it's a long and winding journey, composed of thousands upon thousands of teeny, tiny baby steps throughout an entire lifetime, but when you achieve it, you have found the ultimate form of beauty.

Once you find your genuine beauty, everyone else will see it too. When we think of people we miss, it's always their authenticity we remember.

Be careful online.

"The body is an instrument; Not an ornament."
(Unknown)

Who is choosing your thoughts when you're looking at photos on social media? Marketers are savvy, and they know your insecurities. Who is benefiting from the war inside you? Once you train the mind, you look at people and places in a whole different light. We stop making false assumptions and become more curious. We ask questions. The biggest question you should ask yourself and search for is: **Who am I designed to be?**

Unleash Your Beauty.

What beauty are you bringing into the world? Will you write the loveliest poem? Will you paint the next Monet? Will you help a lonely old lady? Will you start a nonprofit? Will you invent something that saves lives?

If you're always trying to fit an image, you'll never know how awesome you can be. We are given such a short amount of time on this earth. Do you want to have prettier teeth or a prettier soul? Balance your time, so the interior has an advantage over the exterior.

Your so-called "flaws" limit you from reaching your full potential if you let them outweigh your inner beauty. Do something positive with each flaw. Turn them into light. If you think you're "too fat," start a blog about fashion for plus-size women.

You'll find there are lot more girls out there, bigger and happier than you. If you want to lose weight, start a weight loss journey. Make it fun.

Don't dwell on the flaw. One "flaw" doesn't ruin the entire package. You would never throw away a scratched diamond. You would polish it. For 30 days, find something positive about your flaw. Have an enormous nose? Well, did you know big noses give you better protection against bacteria and infections? And people find them culturally expressive. If you still want to change it after that, then, by all means, do some research and find a plastic surgeon. Being truthful about why the flaw bothers you will help you fix it. Most of the time, it's because you're comparing yourself to an image the media has portrayed to you as beautiful or someone who rejected you. Both things heal in time if we work on what's important with the time we're given. We all get lost throughout our busy lives, and a lot of us default to autopilot. We forget about all the little blessings, and we tuck away the goals we want in our subconscious, and they stay there.

Consider beauty as a philosophy.

Look in a full-size mirror. What is the very first thing that comes to your mind? If it's not positive, you still have work. How can you correct the negative thought? Who were you, around five and six years old? Your most innocent age. What did you like to do? What made you feel good? If you really do the work on the inside, your cosmetics will work double time on the outside. Live a life of self-discovery. There is a lesson in almost every situation: People that feel ugly haven't found that spark of beauty inside.

REMEMBER: Beauty is how you change your world and bring out the qualities that lie dormant within you. The past is part of your beauty. No one has your story. There may be similarities in stories, but no one shares your unique journey or gifts.

> *"Life is the most difficult exam. Many people fail beauty when they try to copy others, not realizing everyone has a different questioned paper."*
> *-Unknown*

We all make mistakes. We all have insecurities and completely break down. But it is beauty that mends the broken heart. Beauty is the light inside, our strength. Once we find our unique beauty, it transforms us. We realize life is beautiful, and we are a part of that beauty. Our beauty needs to be shared.

My wish for you is that you ignite the soul of who you are and don't miss any wonders in your individual experience. May you build up all that life has to offer you, and it radiates so much within that when you walk through a door, the essence of who you are (beauty) turns every head. May your genuine beauty generate stares in wonderment and cause people to ask themselves, *"Is she wearing cosmetics or confidence?"* And you'll wink—and that wink will say it all. *"I am walking in my own BEAUTY."*

ABOUT THE AUTHOR

Lisa D'Anna's motto for life is "Don't rest, or you'll rust." If you catch her at a party, she is the girl pulling everyone to the dance floor. She is an apprentice to life and a sales and communications specialist with twenty years of experience. Ten of those years were in the cosmetic field, which inspired the writing of this book.

Lisa lives in Santa Barbara, CA, with her husband and her daughter. She has a degree in marketing, economics and is certified in neurolinguistic programming. She has been studying the mind-body connection for as long as she can remember and has learned first-hand from her unique experiences that confidence is an inside job. Her mission in life is to inspire every single one of us to take the time to discover our God-given gifts and share them with the world.

REFERENCES

Aesthetics, Amy Wechsler Dermatology, New York City |. Dermatology &. "Dr. Amy Wechsler Dermatology, New York City | Dermatology & Aesthetics." *Dr. Amy Wechsler Dermatology*, https://www.dramywechsler.com.

Contributors to Wikimedia projects. "Edward R. Murrow - Wikipedia." *Wikipedia, the Free Encyclopedia*, Wikimedia Foundation, Inc., 3 Dec. 2002, https://en.wikipedia.org/wiki/Edward_R._Murrow.

Doidge, Norman. *The Brain That Changes Itself.* Penguin, 2007.

"Frontiers | Which Body Would You Like to Have? The Impact of Embodied Perspective on Body Perception and Body Evaluation in Immersive Virtual Reality | Robotics and AI." *Frontiers*, https://www.frontiersin.org/articles/10.3389/frobt.2020.00031/full.

"Get the Facts | National Organization for Women." *National Organization for Women*, https://now.org/now-foundation/love-your-body/love-your-body-whats-it-all-about/get-the-facts/.

Gluck, Didi. "How Your Emotions Affect Your Skin | Shape." *Shape*, Shape, 28 Jan. 2019, https://www.shape.com/lifestyle/mind-and-body/how-emotions-affect-skin.

"Helix - Population Genomics." *Helix*, https://www.helix.com. ("Helix - Population Genomics")

Hinshaw, Stephen P., and Rachel Kranz. *The Triple Bind*. Random House Digital, Inc., 2009.

Judging a Book by its Cover: Beauty and Expectations in the Trust Game
Rick K. Wilson and Catherine C. Eckel *Political Research Quarterly* 2006; 59; 189 DOI: 10.1177/106591290605900202
Kolk, Bessel A. Van. *The Body Keeps the Score*. Penguin, 2014.

McLeod, S. A. (2018, May 03). *Erik Erikson's stages of psychosocial development*. Simply Psychology. https://www.simplypsychology.org/Erik-Erikson.html
"Meditation: Good for the Brain, Good for the Skin Too - Mindful." *Mindful*, 30 Aug. 2012, https://www.mindful.org/meditation-good-for-the-brain-good-for-the-skin-too/.

"Ornamental Indoor Plants in Hospital Rooms Enhanced Health Outcomes of Patients Recovering from Surgery - PubMed." *PubMed*, https://pubmed.ncbi.nlm.nih.gov/19715461/.

Palmer, Carl L., and Rolfe Daus Peterson. "Physical Attractiveness, Halo Effects, and Social Joining." *Social Science Quarterly*, no. 1, Wiley, Nov. 2020, pp. 552–66. *Crossref*, doi:10.1111/ssqu.12892.

Political Research Quarterly

http://prq.sagepub.com

The online version of this article can be found at:

http://prq.sagepub.com/cgi/content/abstract/59/2/189

---. "Post-Traumatic Growth - Wikipedia." *Wikipedia, the Free Encyclopedia*, Wikimedia Foundation, Inc., 3 Dec. 2008, https://en.wikipedia.org/wiki/Post-traumatic_growth.

Reuell, Peter. "Rapid Acts of Kindness – Harvard Gazette." *Harvard Gazette*, Harvard Gazette, 20 Sept. 2012, https://news.harvard.edu/gazette/story/2012/09/rapid-acts-of-kindness/.

Sandoiu, Ana. "Why Depression, Trauma Can Make You Age Faster." *Medical and Health Information*, Medical News Today, 9 Oct. 2018, https://www.medicalnewstoday.com/articles/323290.

"Super Longevity: How Meditation Increases Life Span – EOC Institute." *EOC Institute – Access Deep Meditation Quickly, Safely, & Easily*, https://eocinstitute.org/meditation/4-top-ways-meditation-is-the-best-anti-aging-longevity-tool/?152346.

"The Compassionate Mind – Association for Psychological Science – APS." *Association for Psychological Science - APS*, https://www.psychologicalscience.org/observer/the-compassionate-mind.

"The Effects of Aging on Skin: Dry Skin, Loose Skin, and More." *WebMD*, WebMD, 5AD, https://www.webmd.com/beauty/cosmetic-procedures-aging-skin#1.

"The European Centre for Environment & Human Health - European Centre for Environment and Human Health | ECEHH." *European Centre for Environment and Human Health | ECEHH*, https://www.ecehh.org.

"The Wine Project: Three Glasses, Three Pictures — Chel Loves Wine." *Chel Loves Wine*, Chel Loves Wine, 25 Apr. 2016, https://www.chelloveswine.com/blog/wine-project.

Wechsler, Amy. *The Mind-Beauty Connection*. Simon and Schuster, 2008.

"Welcome to EMDR.Com - EMDR Institute - EYE MOVEMENT DESENSITIZATION AND REPROCESSING THERAPY." *EMDR Institute - EYE MOVEMENT DESENSITIZATION AND REPROCESSING THERAPY*, https://www.emdr.com.

"What Did David Letterman Do to the Late Show Studio? - Profound Journey." *Profound Journey*, 18 Oct. 2016, https://profoundjourney.com/david-letterman-lowered-temperature-late-show-studio/.

Zondervan. *NIV, Holy Bible, Economy Edition, Paperback, Comfort Print*. 2020.

Made in United States
North Haven, CT
09 April 2023

35219881R00076